CCH® Basic Employment Law Manual for Managers and Supervisors

Third Edition

Paul C. Gibson, J.D.
Kathryn S. Piscitelli, J.D.

Wolters Kluwer
Law & Business

Contributing Editors: Susan Cumming, J.D., Joyce Gentry, J.D., Brett Gorovsky, J.D., Deborah Hammonds, J.D., Kathleen Kapusta, J.D., Martha Pedrick, J.D., David Stephanides, J.D., Joy Waltemath, J.D., Pam Wolf, J.D.

Book Production Coordinator: Danford A. Miller.

This publication is designed to provide accurate and authoritative information in regard to the subject matter covered. It is sold with the understanding that the publisher is not engaged in rendering legal, accounting or other professional service. If legal advice or other expert assistance is required, the services of a competent professional person should be sought.

ISBN 0-8080-1488-9

© 2006, CCH. All Rights Reserved
4025 W. Peterson Ave.
Chicago, IL 60646-6085
1 800 248 3248
hr.cch.com

Printed in the United States of America

Introduction

Hear the wake-up call

Hardly a week goes by without the media reporting that a company is being sued for employment law violations. Indeed, employment law cases continue to increase—so much so, in fact, that employment lawsuits continue to be one of the fastest-growing types of litigation. In particular, the last few years have seen a veritable "explosion" in class action litigation over workplace issues, including employment discrimination and wage-hour issues. Over 75,000 charges against employers were filed in fiscal year 2005 with the Equal Employment Opportunity Commission, the agency that enforces the federal employment discrimination laws. Those charges potentially can wind up in court.

The costs to an organization sued for employment law violations can be staggering. Whether instituted by a government agency or filed by a private party, the combined costs of settlements topped $1.4 billion in 2005, according to published reports. For example, the EEOC reports collecting as much as $450,000 for individual sexual harassment plaintiffs and settling a class action against a retailer requiring the establishment of a $40 million fund for victims of race, color, national origin and sex discrimination..

Given this pervasive legal climate, it remains crucial for managers and supervisors to be aware of the legal issues surrounding their dealings with employees. This Third Edition of *Basic Employment Law Manual for Managers and Supervisors* provides a basic understanding of how the employment laws impact issues that managers and supervisors face every day in their jobs. The book is designed to be a handy reference to help you as a manager or supervisor in complying with these laws.

Take action to avoid liability

Managers and supervisors must take action to avoid lawsuits. This book provides managers and supervisors with guidance that will help to prevent lawsuits and to reduce the risk of liability if their company is sued.

Key actions that the book teaches managers and supervisors to take to stay out of legal trouble include the following:

- Learn what the employment laws are and what rights and protections employees have under them.
- Use only job-related factors as the basis for employment decisions.
- Apply work rules in the same way to all employees.
- Treat people as individuals and in a respectful manner that recognizes the valuable contribution each person makes to the organization.
- Use performance appraisals and discipline not as punishment, but as positive tools for improving employee job performance or conduct.
- Give employees honest, accurate feedback.
- Never discipline or terminate someone without first checking out whether doing so is fair, legal, nonretaliatory, and consistent with organization policies.
- Document employees' performance.
- Watch what you say:

— Don't make rude or discriminatory remarks.

— Don't make employment promises.

— Don't interpret benefit plans.

— Don't make false or mean comments about employees.

— Don't discuss disciplinary issues concerning an employee except with persons who have a legitimate right to know.

— Don't broadcast private facts about an employee.

— Don't respond to a reference check without first checking organization policy.

— Don't threaten employees who engage in union activity, or any other protected activity.

• Take seriously employees' complaints about harassment, misconduct, wages, hours, job conditions, injuries, and organization practices that may harm the public or violate the law.

Be a good manager

The principles covered in this book are not just useful in avoiding lawsuits; they also serve as basic steps to good human resources management. People management in general, including disciplinary action, should be viewed as the process of building a work force of productive persons. Use the information in this book first, to be a good manager or supervisor and second, to keep your company out of legal trouble.

August 2006

ACKNOWLEDGEMENTS

CCH gratefully thanks the following persons for their generous assistance with the original edition of this project:

José De La Cruz

Regional Employee Resources Manager

Southeastern United States

Pfizer Inc. - U.S. Pharmaceuticals Group

Atlanta, Georgia

Paula Ann Hughes, Ph.D., SPHR

Dean

Graduate School of Management

University of Dallas

Irving, Texas

Edward J. Kelly

Assistant to the President

Brockport State College

Brockport, New York

G. Roger King

Partner

Jones, Day, Reavis and Pogue

Columbus, Ohio

Lynn C. Outwater, Attorney

Jackson, Lewis, Schnitzler & Krupman

Pittsburgh, Pennsylvania

John A. Ricca

Assistant Vice President and

Assistant General Counsel

Fireman's Fund Insurance Company

Novato, California

John A. Young, SPHR

Manager of Human Resources

Bailey Transportation Products

Conneaut, Ohio

Table of Contents

8

Overview of Employment Laws

FEDERAL LAWS

Key federal employment laws that managers and supervisors should know about include the following:

Title VII of the Civil Rights Act of 1964 (Title VII). Title VII prohibits discrimination on the basis of race, color, religion, sex, or national origin.

Age Discrimination in Employment Act of 1967 (ADEA). The ADEA bans discrimination on the basis of age against persons who are 40 or older.

Americans with Disabilities Act of 1990 (ADA). The ADA forbids discrimination against qualified individuals with disabilities. The ADA also requires that reasonable accommodations be made to the known physical or mental limitations of qualified applicants or employees.

Equal Pay Act of 1963 (EPA). Paying workers of one sex at a rate different from that paid to the other sex violates the EPA when jobs involve equal skill, effort, and responsibility *and* are performed under similar working conditions in the same establishment.

Immigration Reform and Control Act of 1986 (IRCA). IRCA prohibits discrimination on the basis of citizenship against persons who have a legal right to work in this country. (IRCA also requires employers to verify that all new hires are authorized to work in the United States. Human Resources departments usually handle this task.)

Family and Medical Leave Act of 1993 (FMLA). The FMLA guarantees an employee up to 12 weeks of job-protected, unpaid leave each year for any one or more of the following reasons:

- the birth or adoption of a child
- the serious health condition of a child, spouse, or parent
- the employee's own serious illness or pregnancy

Uniformed Services Employment and Reemployment Rights Act of 1994 (USERRA). USERRA bans discrimination on the basis of past, current, or future military service. It also provides for military leaves of absence and reemployment of employees after military leave.

National Labor Relations Act (NLRA). The NLRA gives employees the right to unionize, the right to bargain collectively, and the right to engage in other activities for their mutual aid and protection.

Sarbanes-Oxley Act of 2002 (SOX). SOX gives whistleblower protection to employees of publicly traded companies who provide information to governmental authorities about conduct they believe to be mail, wire, securities or shareholder fraud.

STATE LAWS

Statutes. Most states have employment laws that provide the same rights as those provided under the federal statutes discussed above. Some state employment laws grant even greater rights. For instance, discrimination on the basis of sexual orientation, political affiliation, marital status, nursing mother status, genetic information, or off-duty conduct may be prohibited under state legislation.

Common law. State common law (court-created law) is yet another source of employee rights. Below are some state common law theories under which an employee may sue a company:

- *Infliction of emotional distress*—the employee suffered severe emotional distress as a result of abusive treatment in the workplace.

- *Defamation*—a false or malicious statement (either written or spoken) was made about the employee that resulted in damage to the employee's reputation.

- *Invasion of privacy*—a supervisor publicly disclosed private facts about the employee, such as the details of a performance appraisal.

- *Interference with employment*—a supervisor tried to get the employee fired—or to botch his or her chances of getting or keeping a new job—in order to gain personal revenge or advantage.

- *Fraud or negligent misrepresentation*—the employee suffered harm as a result of reliance on false statements made to the employee about job security, performance evaluations, health hazards, or some other employment matter.

- *Negligent employment*—the employee was injured by a co-worker whom the company knew or should have known could harm others.

- *False imprisonment*—the employee was detained or restrained against the employee's will.

- *Battery*—the employee was subjected to harmful or offensive contact.

- *Assault*—the employee was threatened with harmful or offensive contact.

- *Constructive discharge*—the employee resigned in response to working conditions that the employee found intolerable.

- *Discharge in violation of public policy*—the employee was fired for exercising a legal right, such as filing a workers' compensation claim; for satisfying a legal obligation, such as serving on a jury or making a required court appearance; or for reporting or protesting the company's illegal conduct.

- *Breach of contract*—an explicit written or spoken employment-related promise (such as a formal agreement to employ the employee for a set number of years) was broken.

- *Breach of implied contract*—an implicit employment-related promise (such as a supervisor's comments implying job security for the employee, or a personnel handbook statement implying that specific disciplinary procedures will be followed before anyone is fired) was broken.

VIOLATIONS ARE COSTLY

Court-ordered penalties. Remedies that courts may order for violations of employment rights include:

- Rehiring of someone who was illegally fired.

- Hiring of an applicant who was illegally refused employment.

- Back pay (payment of wages to an illegally fired employee for the period he or she was out of work).

- Double back pay for willful violations of certain laws.

- Front pay (payment of future wages that would have been earned if an employee had not been illegally fired.)

- Compensatory damages for losses suffered as a result of illegal conduct. Losses that a company may be ordered to pay for include:

  Nonmonetary losses (emotional pain, suffering, inconvenience, mental anguish, loss of enjoyment of life);

  Future monetary losses (expected losses due to inability to work, future medical expenses); and

  Past monetary losses (doctor's bills, money spent in seeking another job).

- Punitive damages to punish severe violations.
- Payment of an employee's attorney and expert witness fees.

Other consequences. Violations of the employment laws can also result in:

- Lost productive time of persons involved in resolving claims of unlawful conduct.
- Low employee morale.
- High employee turnover.
- Harm to the company's reputation and business.
- Government involvement in the company's business practices.

CAN MANAGERS OR SUPERVISORS BE LIABLE?

Personal liability of managers and supervisors under the federal employment laws is a hotly debated issue that remains unresolved. A number of courts have said only employers can be held liable. But others have concluded that managers and supervisors can be required to pay for their own illegal conduct.

However, regardless of their liability under the federal laws, managers and supervisors can still be held personally liable when their conduct violates state common law (such as assault, battery, intentional infliction of emotional distress). Employees can also be made to pay for their own common law violations.

Discrimination/Fairness

KNOW WHICH GROUPS ARE PROTECTED FROM DISCRIMINATION

Awareness and knowledge are the keys to avoiding employment discrimination. Each supervisor or line manager—the management person with the most direct contact with employees—must be familiar with the types of discrimination that are not permitted in the workplace.

Federal laws. Federal equal employment opportunity (EEO) laws prohibit employers from basing employment decisions on any of the following personal traits that may apply to an applicant or employee:

- Race or color
- Religion
- Sex (includes sexual harassment, equal pay, and pregnancy)
- Age (applies generally to persons age 40 or over)
- Disability (physical or mental)
- National origin
- Citizenship status (applies to U.S. citizens or aliens who are authorized to work in the U.S.)
- Veteran or military status

State laws. Some state EEO laws also prohibit discrimination on the basis of:

- Arrest records
- Marital status
- Sexual orientation
- State of residency
- Political affiliation
- Lawful off-duty activities
- Lactation
- Genetic information

HOW DISCRIMINATION OCCURS

Job discrimination exists when employees or applicants who are members of a protected group are treated less favorably than others.

Intentional discrimination ("disparate treatment"). Unlawful discrimination is usually the result of a deliberate intent to base an employment decision on a person's protected status.

To avoid charges of intentional discrimination, managers and supervisors must:

1. Use only job-related factors as the basis for employment decisions—whether decisions about hiring, transfers, promotions, discipline, layoffs, terminations, pay, or job environment.

2. Never base an employment decision on a person's membership in a protected group.

3. Treat employees consistently and fairly.

Unintentional discrimination ("disparate impact"). Unlawful discrimination can also occur in the absence of any discriminatory intent. Unintentional discrimination takes place when a job requirement (such as a test, diploma, or height requirement) that applies to all employees tends to exclude members of a protected group. Such a requirement is against the law if it is not job-related and is not necessary to the business. If you think a company requirement is unfairly screening out members of a protected group, you should notify your Human Resources department.

DISCRIMINATORY SITUATIONS

1. Discharging older workers and hiring younger, lower-paid workers. Workers 40 years of age and older are protected from employment discrimination on the basis of age.

2. Requiring workers to speak English in the workplace. Unless the employer can prove sound business or safety reasons why it needs to bar the use of a language other than English, it cannot do so.

3. Disciplining an employee for not working on a religious holiday. Employers are obligated to accommodate the religious needs of employees up to the point of undue hardship, and employees are required to minimize the potential conflicts.

4. Firing a minority employee for poor job performance where the poor performance can be traced to a racially motivated failure to provide the worker with the proper training to perform the job.

5. Firing an employee for absenteeism without determining whether the absenteeism was due to racially or sexually offensive conduct on the part of the employee's coworkers.

6. Early retirement plans—retirement must be totally voluntary and give a reasonable amount of time for employees to decide whether to retire early.

7. Terminating employees due to relocation of a facility while offering jobs at the new location to similarly situated members of another class . . . or offering relocation or commuting assistance to members of one class but not to members of another class.

8. Refusing to hire a qualified applicant because of the need to accommodate that person's disability. An employer must provide a reasonable accommodation to the known physical or mental limitations of qualified disabled applicants unless it can prove that the accommodation would impose an undue hardship on its business.

9. Firing a woman because she is pregnant.

10. Discharging minority employees, employees of one sex, or older employees in such large numbers that it can be shown that there is a pattern of discharging only workers who are protected by EEO laws.

11. Refusing to hire a reservist because the reservist's military obligations may conflict with work.

12. Firing an employee who has lodged a discrimination complaint or participated in the investigation of discrimination charges.

APPLY RULES AND STANDARDS FAIRLY

Managers and supervisors are "the company" to most workers. That is, people may shape their opinion of an entire company based, in large part, on the day-to-day relationship they have with their manager or supervisor. If people are treated unfairly by their immediate managers or supervisors, they will come to believe that the company is unfair and a bad place to work. Lawsuits are likely to result. It is thus important that managers apply workplace rules and performance standards fairly.

There are two important elements to workplace fairness—

1. Respond to similar situations in a consistent fashion.

2. Treat people as individuals and in a respectful manner that recognizes the valuable contribution each person makes to the company.

CONSISTENT APPLICATION OF RULES IS BASIC TO FAIRNESS

Managers and supervisors must apply work rules and work standards consistently. If it looks like something is being done in one case but not another, people may assign improper motives to the action, even if no such motive was present.

The following actual cases show how companies got in trouble when work rules were not applied in a consistent fashion—

Example 1:: A black employee was fired for insubordination when she refused to stay late for overtime. The employee was able to show race discrimination since white employees who left at the regular quitting time on the same day were not disciplined.

Example 2:: An employer engaged in "reverse discrimination" when firing a white employee for theft of cargo while retaining a black worker who was involved in similar misconduct.

Example 3:: Firing a female machine operator was discriminatory, even though the operator violated unwritten safety regulations, because males usually operated the same machinery in a similar fashion.

"Don'ts" for supervisors. To avoid inconsistency:

* Don't play favorites by constantly giving favorable assignments to the same individuals.

* Don't issue a warning to one employee who has broken a company rule and ignore the same conduct of another employee.

* Don't document to build a case only against troublemakers or people you want to fire. Document good performance as well as poor performance.

AVOID RETALIATION

Applicants, employees and even former employees are generally protected under employment laws from a wide range of retaliatory acts by employers. Retaliation is unlawful when it is directed against an individual who has engaged in protected activity, like asserting a statutorily-protected right, opposing a prohibited employment practice, or participating in a statutorily-authorized investigation or proceeding. Since anyone can oppose unlawful discrimination and participate in proceedings intended to stop discrimination, the retaliation ban can protect individuals who were not themselves victims of the original claimed discrimination.

What types of employer conduct can be considered illegal retaliation? To be unlawful, retaliatory action must be something that an objectively reasonable employee would find "materially adverse;" in other words, significant enough that it is "likely to dissuade employees from complaining or assisting in complaints about discrimination." Prohibited retaliation can even include actions not directly related to employment or that cause harm outside of the workplace. Often retaliation charges come up when an employer wants to discipline an employee for some action or inaction. Consequently, managers and supervisors must review all of the circumstances surrounding the proposed discipline, keeping in mind a checklist of activities against which employers cannot retaliate.

To reduce the likelihood that employees who claim discrimination or otherwise participate in asserting such rights will file retaliation charges:

- **Avoid unequal treatment.** Treat employees who have claimed discrimination or participated in proceedings on behalf of claimants the same as individuals who participate in such proceedings on behalf of the employer.

- **Establish an independent basis for discipline.** If discipline is warranted, it can never be based an employee's participation in protected proceedings. Since unlawful motive is the key, be careful not to create an appearance of unlawful motive.

- **Don't try to limit participation rights.** Promises not to file a charge or participate in proceedings should not be included in contracts requiring the use of alternative dispute resolution procedures, waiver agreements, employee handbooks, employee benefit plans, and noncompete agreements. First, these promises are generally not enforceable, and second, they may also amount to independent violations of the anti-retaliation provisions of employment laws.

TREAT PEOPLE KINDLY AND RESPECTFULLY

Kind, respectful treatment of employees will improve their performance and reduce the chance of discipline problems. How can a manager or supervisor focus on treating employees kindly and respectfully? Follow these tips:

- Ask how you would like to be treated by your boss. Then treat people working with you accordingly.
- Let people know what is expected of them as employees.
- Don't make unreasonable demands.
- Make work assignments in a courteous manner.
- Take the time to explain why the work people do is important.
- Stop to ask people for their help in solving problems.
- Make people feel valuable. Take time to thank them for their contribution.

Supervisor Statements as Evidence

SUPERVISORS' STATEMENTS BECOME EVIDENCE IN COURT

Statements made by supervisors or managers often become key parts of a court case alleging that an employee was unlawfully fired. The statements are used by employees to show that a company had unlawful motivations for a firing or that a situation existed that unfairly forced the employee to resign. Here are some examples of statements made by supervisors that wound up being used as evidence to show that a termination was improper—

- Calling female employees *"girls"* while referring to male employees as "men" was evidence of both race and sex discrimination. The term "girl" could refer to a repulsive historical image in the minds of black employees and could also imply to women historical attitudes of female inferiority.

- A supervisor's *religious preaching* at the workplace showed that an employer failed to provide a workplace free of religious intimidation. Employees could believe that job security would be affected by their reaction to the supervisor's statements of religious belief.

- A manager's statement at a business dinner to a female coworker that he had heard that she had been seen engaging in *sexual activity* with another woman was sexual harassment.

- Remarks by supervisors referring to a Chinese worker as a *"chink"* and as *"tight eye"* were the main pieces of evidence used by a court to find that a racially hostile work environment existed that unlawfully forced the worker to resign.

- Statements made by a supervisor at the *social setting* of a holiday dinner were used to show that an employee was not fired for poor performance. The supervisor praised the employee's work, indicated that she was an excellent employee and requested at least five years' notice if the employee ever planned to leave the company. The employee claimed she was fired due to her age, and used the statements to rebut the company's claim that poor performance was the reason for the termination.

- A supervisor's frequent *remarks about black employees* that included such language as "niggers" and "swahilis" were used by a court to find a racially hostile workplace.

- A remark by a supervisor that "the lousy liberal *Jews are ruining the company* and the United States," along with the supervisor's expression of anger that a Jewish employee, in observance of his religion, left work early on Fridays to arrive home before sundown, could be used in court to show that the employee was forced to resign because of his religion.

- Remarks that college recruits had "very high" energy levels and were "very open *to learning new techniques*" were sufficient evidence to allow a $110,000 jury award to a man who claimed he was fired due to age bias.

- A manager's use of the phrase *"old dogs don't know how to hunt"* could indirectly suggest that a 63-year-old employee was not fired because of declining performance.

- Statements that an employee would need to have "vision," embrace "new technology" and be *"state of the art"* raised an issue as to whether a company's reasons for replacing the 54-year-old employee were a pretext for age discrimination.

- Performance evaluation statements that described a female accountant as "macho," advised her to *"take a course in charm school"* and suggested that she "overcompensated for being a woman" showed that the employer improperly engaged in stereotyping that amounted to sexual discrimination against the woman.

SUPERVISORS' PROMISES CAN CREATE CONTRACTS

Supervisors' promises to employees may be interpreted by courts as enforceable employment contracts. Following are examples of the types of supervisor statements that employees have alleged to create binding contracts—

- Statements made by a supervisor in annual reviews that "I am glad you work here and *hope we will have many more years working together*" and that the supervisor "desired a long-term working relationship" could have created an employment contract.

- Because an employee was told that he would be promoted within six months of starting a job and that he would *receive an annual salary* and a specific vacation period, the employee was entitled to have a jury decide whether those statements created an employment contract for a specified period of time.

- Statements that an employee could *expect job security as long as he did his job* and that he could expect a promotion if he did a good job were evidence that a contract of employment was created.

- A statement in an interview that potential employees did not have to worry about their jobs *as long as the job gets done* could be evidence of an offer of permanent employment.

- An employee used his supervisor's statement that *"we will retire together"* to allege in court that he had a lifetime employment contract.

SUPERVISORS SHOULD NOT INTERPRET BENEFIT PLANS

While it is the duty of a supervisor to know what the benefits policy of the employer is, it is not the supervisor's job to handle inquiries regarding that policy. Questioners should be directed first to the employee benefit handbook and then to the benefits administrator. The supervisor should make sure that each employee has a copy of the benefits plan and keep employees informed about any changes in the plan. However, the supervisor should in no way attempt to interpret the plan's provisions for employees. Any such interpretation could become an enforceable oral modification to that plan.

SUPERVISORS SPEAK FOR THE COMPANY

The **key lesson** to be learned from the above examples is that statements made by supervisors can be directly attributed to their company. Supervisors are considered to be **agents** of the company. Any statements made by a supervisor can be attributed to the employer and used as evidence to show that a company acted improperly. Thus, supervisors should be careful that their statements relate only to their job of managing people to meet company goals.

Documentation

WHY USE DOCUMENTATION?

There are several important reasons that a manager or supervisor should document actions taken while managing people:

1. Evidence. Documentation is an essential element of any human resources program. Personnel decisions are less subject to challenge and, when challenged, are more easily defended with documentation. In court cases, unemployment hearings, and grievance arbitration, if a company's documentation is not timely, accurate and written to correct the problem, the company is likely to lose.

2. Performance improvement. Documentation can provide a written set of goals or objectives that an employee must meet to improve performance. A written set of performance goals or standards can prevent misunderstandings about what an employee must accomplish to improve performance.

3. Communication. The process of ongoing review and dialogue should be part of the manager/employee relationship. The use of documentation can improve feedback between a manager and an employee.

4. A record for personnel actions. When managers need to substantiate their actions to others they use documentation. In the event that an evaluation, pay raise, or disciplinary action is questioned, documentation will be the key to supporting that action.

5. Notice to the employee. Documentation provides evidence that an employee was actually or constructively aware of the rules, verification that the employee heard and understood the rules and policies, and evidence that policies have been consistently applied and enforced. Documentation will help to support a manager's position that the manager did or did not do something. Generally, employees are not bound by rules that have not been brought to their attention, nor should they be punished for conduct that they did not reasonably understand was a problem.

6. Guidelines for future performance. Documentation eliminates any possible misunderstanding concerning work rules. It also allows a manager to state clearly what is expected of an employee in the future and to describe to the employee the consequences of future infractions. For example, when a manager becomes aware of unsatisfactory performance, documentation can provide evidence that an employee was accorded progressive discipline, was adequately warned about poor performance, and had a reasonable opportunity to improve.

7. Training and development. Documentation can also be used as a record of an employee's training and development, how an employee performed during training, and the employee's career goals.

THE ROLE OF DOCUMENTATION IN DISCIPLINE/ TERMINATIONS

When disciplinary or termination decisions are being made, documentation is especially critical for several reasons—

1. Adhering to company policies. Documentation can indicate whether an employee knew that the policy existed and whether a manager warned the employee about violating the policy. It can also show whether there were any mitigating circumstances and whether the manager followed company policies and procedures when disciplining the employee.

2. A valid business purpose. Documentation will provide evidence that a valid business purpose exists for the disciplinary or termination action, as well as show that the action does not violate any statute, policy, or specific employment agreement.

3. Evenhanded treatment. Documentation can provide evidence that employees who have engaged in similar conduct were subject to similar discipline, thus supporting the position that an employee's protected status (race, color, religion, sex, national origin, age, disability, etc.) had nothing to do with the termination decision.

4. Accommodation. If accommodation is an issue, documentation can provide evidence that an employer made an offer of reasonable accommodation, taking into account a person's religion or disability.

5. Investigation. It is important to conduct a thorough investigation prior to any disciplinary or termination decision. The use of documentation can provide evidence that such an investigation was conducted and employees were given the opportunity to relate their side of the story.

6. Creating a record. An employee's overall personnel record should support the disciplinary or termination decision. Thorough documentation can provide such evidence and substantiate the fact that an employee was told how to improve when he or she needed to improve and what the consequence of failing to improve would be.

CASE ILLUSTRATION

The following case shows how managers can set standards and document whether employees are meeting those standards:

A 55-year-old manager was fired after new management took over a chain of retail stores. The manager claimed that she was fired because of her age. She showed that she had a long history of successful performance with the company and that she had been promoted several times. The employer was able to prove that it had enforced higher standards of performance to improve its stores and the manager was not meeting those new, higher standards. The employer, by documenting each of the manager's failures and warning her repeatedly, was able to prove every aspect of its case against her.

DOCUMENT COMMUNICATIONS WITH ALL EMPLOYEES

Documentation should be a standard practice. Similar job-related communications should be documented for all employees. This includes both negative and positive occurrences. The documentation process should not be used to build a case against one employee if other employees in similar situations did not have their actions documented. Inconsistent documentation may be proof that a person was chosen for discharge for unlawful reasons.

FAILURE TO DOCUMENT CAN GET A COMPANY IN TROUBLE

A supervisor's failure to document may lead to an inference of discrimination. It places a company in a position of not being able to adequately defend itself against claims that it is treating some employees differently.

It also has a negative impact on employee relations. Employees often become poor performers simply because there is no communication between their supervisors and them. The employees are led to believe that their conduct or performance is satisfactory when, in fact, it is unsatisfactory. Only when a supervisor gets "fed up" or frustrated will performance discussion take place with an employee. By that time, it may be too late and the company may lose a valuable employee.

DOCUMENTATION SHOULD GIVE DETAILS

Avoid making broad, general statements when documenting an employee's performance. Instead, deal with the facts, be specific, and tell the story. For example, don't say: "Susie lied." Give details about the false statement: "Susie said she couldn't come to work on Friday because her car broke down. I asked her for receipts for repairs. She couldn't provide them. I asked her for the name of the garage where the repairs were allegedly done and she couldn't remember."

DOCUMENTATION SHOULD BE TIMELY

Timeliness is critical. Delay or inaction in documenting an incident can be construed as a waiver of a supervisor's right to take any action regarding that incident.

THE EMPLOYEE SHOULD BE GIVEN A COPY

It is a good idea to give the employee a copy of the documentation. Giving the employee a copy will ensure that the employee is on notice of what is wrong and what must be changed.

Benefits

SUPERVISORS SHOULDN'T GIVE ADVICE ON BENEFIT QUESTIONS

The best advice a line manager or supervisor can give an employee regarding benefits and termination is no advice at all. There is an enormous potential for well-meaning comments made by a supervisor to lead to litigation. Although the law requires employee benefit plans to be in writing, ambiguous written provisions can be changed based on statements made by company officials. That means that if a plan does not precisely spell out what will happen in a given termination situation and the supervisor, in answering an employee question, interprets the plan to provide benefits where none were intended, the employer could end up being sued for not paying benefits.

The answer to questions like "Will I get severance pay if the company is sold and I continue to work for the new owner?" or "Will my health insurance coverage continue while I look for a new job after the plant closes?" should be either "Consult your employee handbook" or "See the benefits administrator." The handbook and the benefits administrator should be the only sources of communication regarding benefits issues.

TELL PEOPLE TO CHECK BENEFIT PLAN DOCUMENTS

Senior management's role is to make sure that the company's termination policy and benefit plan documents are properly drafted. The supervisor's job is to see that all employees are aware of the policy and the plan. The supervisor should be able to say with confidence: "That question is addressed in your benefits booklet" or "You should seek information from the benefits administrator." This will avoid putting the supervisor on the spot to answer questions and avoid having the supervisor interpret the plan.

WHAT CAN GO WRONG WITH SUPERVISOR BENEFIT STATEMENTS

Here is an example of what can go wrong when a well-meaning supervisor attempts to interpret a benefits plan:

> Company A has decided to sell one of its divisions. A buyer has been found that is going to hire all of the Company A employees. The Company A severance policy contains words that can be interpreted in different ways. It states that any employee who is *terminated for reasons other than cause* will get one week of pay for every year of service with the company.

> The above words can have a couple of meanings in this situation. They can be read to mean that the employees will be entitled to severance pay since they are being terminated by Company A and will work for the buyer. At the same time, it can just as easily be argued that no severance pay is required since the employees are not losing their jobs when the buyer agrees to immediately hire them. In addition to the ambiguously worded plan, Company A has not designated someone to discuss benefits with employees.

> The employees learn of the sale and start asking their supervisors whether they will get severance pay as a result of changing employers. Several employees go to the plant manager, indicating that they see the change in ownership as a big change in their employment situation. Their question is: "We'll get severance pay, right?" The response from the manager is: "Well,

it seems to me you are going to be terminated and the plan says severance pay will be provided when someone is terminated."

As a result of this discussion on the plant floor, the employer is facing a potential oral interpretation of the ambiguous severance pay policy. The supervisor's statement could be used as evidence to show that the company intended to provide severance pay when there is a change in ownership. That may be a result that the employer did not intend.

TERMINATIONS SHOULD NOT APPEAR TO CUT OFF BENEFITS

A benefit issue involved in individual terminations concerns the employee who is about to have enough service with the company to be eligible for benefits. This is called vesting. Under the Employee Retirement Income Security Act ("ERISA"), it is illegal to discharge an employee solely to prevent that person from vesting or qualifying for benefits.

This problem occurs most often in the following manner. An employee is required to work a given number of years before being eligible to receive benefits. The employee is terminated shortly before fulfilling the time obligation. If the employee can show that the specific intent of the discharge was to stop the eligibility for benefits, the employee has the right to sue to recover the lost benefits.

Because supervisors are often called upon to handle individual terminations, they must be aware of this potential problem. Where it is necessary to terminate an employee and the employee's benefits are about to vest, extra care must be taken to document the reasons for the discharge in order to avoid the appearance that the discharge was a way to avoid paying benefits. While keeping careful records of reviews and employee evaluations is always an important part of a supervisor's duties, that task becomes essential in the context of the suspicious discharge.

Job Interviews

✓ CHECKLIST: PREPARING FOR THE INTERVIEW

Prepare ahead of time for the interview. To help you prepare, use the following checklist.

- ☐ Get a copy of the job description.
- ☐ Familiarize yourself with the duties of the job.
- ☐ Know the promotional potential of the job.
- ☐ Review the applicant's background information.
- ☐ Develop a list of job-related interview questions.
- ☐ Arrange for a suitable place and time for the interview.
- ☐ Allow enough time for the interview.

ASK APPLICANTS JOB-RELATED QUESTIONS ONLY

Interview questions that bear no actual relationship to applicants' ability or qualifications for a job may have the effect of denying employment opportunities to members of protected groups. In choosing interview questions, ask yourself:

1. Will the answer to this question, if used in making a selection, have the effect of screening out members of a protected group?

2. Is this information really needed to judge an applicant's competence or qualifications for the job in question?

QUESTIONS TO AVOID

Race or color. Don't ask.

Sex. Don't ask.

Marital or family status. Don't ask: "Are you married?" "How many children do you have?" "How old are your children?" "Do you plan to have children?" "Are you pregnant?" or "Who will care for your children while you are at work?"

Age or date of birth. Don't ask unless age really is a job requirement. This may be necessary for minimum age requirements, in which case you can ask: "Are you of legal age to work?"

Birthplace, national origin, or ancestry. Don't ask.

Citizenship. Don't ask: "Are you a U.S. citizen?" or "Do you plan to become a U.S. citizen?" However, you may ask: "If hired, can you show that you are eligible to work in the U.S.?"

Residence. Don't ask about an applicant's ownership or rental of a residence or length of residence at an address. However, you may ask: "Where can we reach you?"

Crimes. Don't ask: "Have you ever been arrested or charged with a crime?" or "Have you ever been convicted of a crime?" Your company's Human Resources department will be responsible for asking about crimes and running criminal background checks. However, if there are any gaps in an applicant's employment record, you should ask why he or she was not working during those times. If the applicant says he or she was convicted of a crime, find out: (1) what the crime was; (2) the date of the crime; and (3) whether he or she is subject to any parole requirements that would interfere with performance of the job. Tell the applicant that a conviction won't automatically bar employment, and that the seriousness and date of the crime will be considered. Consult with your Human Resources department about whether the applicant should be rejected.

Health or disabilities. The Americans with Disabilities Act limits employers' ability to make disability-related inquiries or require medical exams at the following stages of the hiring process: (1) during the job interview; and (2) after applicants are given conditional job offers, but before they start work.

Job interview stage. At the job interview stage, an employer may not ask applicants any disability-related questions or require them to take any medical exams, *even if* they are related to the job. Disability-related inquiries are questions that are likely to elicit information about a disability. During this stage, the employer cannot ask applicants questions about their disability, even if: (1) the applicant has voluntarily disclosed their disability status; or (2) the disability is visible to the employer.

Employers should focus on interview questions about non-medical job qualifications designed to determine an applicant's qualifications for a job. At this stage, don't ask: "Do you have any physical or mental disabilities that will keep you from performing this job?" "Do you have a drug or alcohol problem?" or "Have you ever received workers' compensation benefits?" Questions that are not likely to elicit information about a disability are always permitted, like asking about applicants' general well-being. Employer's can also ask: "Given the description of the job duties, can you perform any or all of the job duties with or without reasonable accommodation?" or "Can you meet my attendance requirements?" You can also ask applicants to describe how they will perform any or all of the job duties, as long as *all* applicants for the job are asked to do this.

Medical exams are procedures or tests usually given by a health care professional or in a medical setting that seeks information about an individual's physical or mental impairments or health. They can include vision tests; blood, urine, and breath analyses; blood pressure screening and cholesterol testing; and diagnostic procedures, such as x-rays, CAT scans and MRIs. During the job interview stage there are a number of procedures and tests an employer can perform that generally are not considered medical exams, such as: (1) tests to determine the current illegal use of drugs; (2) physical agility tests (that are not considered medical); (3) psychological tests that measure personality traits such as honest, preferences and habits; and (4) polygraph examinations.

Reasonable accommodations during the interview. Employers are also required to provide applicants who have disabilities with a reasonable accommodation for the job interview if one is requested, like providing applicants' with readers or sign language interpretors. While an employer does not have to provide an accommodation that is of a significant difficulty or expense, the employer cannot refuse to provide an accommodation solely because it entails some costs, either financial or administrative.

Conditional job offers. After an applicant is given a conditional job offer, but before they start work, an employer may ask disability-related questions and conduct medical exams, regardless of whether they are related to the job, as long as the employer does so for *all* entering employees in the same job category. Therefore, at this stage, the employer can ask about the applicants' workers' compensation history, prior sick leave usage, illnesses/diseases/impairments and general physical/mental health.

A job offer is real if the employer has evaluated all relevant nonmedical information which it reasonably could have obtained and analyzed prior to giving the offer.

An employer cannot withdraw a job offer solely because a disability-related question or medical exam reveals that an applicant has a disability. For example, an employer cannot withdraw an offer to an HIV-positive applicant because of concerns about customer and client reactions or because the employer might assume that anyone with HIV will be unable to work long and stressful hours. The employer can only withdraw a job offer if it can be shown that the applicant: (1) was unable to perform any or all of their job duties with or without reasonable accommodation; or (2) posed a significant safety risk. At this stage, managers and supervisors should make sure and consider whether any reasonable accommodations would: (1) enable the applicant to perform the job's essential functions; and/or (2) reduce any safety risk the applicant might pose.

Current or future military service. Don't ask: "Do you have any military obligations?" or "Do you expect to serve in the military?"

Veteran status or military discharge. Don't ask: "Are you a veteran?" or "Were you ever in the military?" Instead, ask: "Do you have any special skills, experience, or training that would qualify you for this job?" Also don't ask: "What kind of military discharge did you receive?" or "Were you ever disciplined in the military?" But if an applicant happens to disclose that he or she was dishonorably discharged under sentence by a court martial, you should proceed as if the applicant had revealed a criminal conviction (see "Crimes," above).

Height and weight. Don't ask unless these standards are essential to the safe performance of the job.

English or foreign language skill. Don't ask unless necessary for the job for which the applicant is applying.

Education. Don't ask whether an applicant has a high school or other specific educational degree unless the degree is a job-related requirement.

Religion/availability to work on weekends or holidays. Don't ask: "Are you active in any church organizations?" or "Do you have the names of any clergy as references?" If you want to know if an applicant can work on weekends or holidays, don't ask: "Does your religion prohibit you from working on any days or at any time?" Instead, ask: "Can you work overtime?" "Can you work weekends?" "Are there any shifts that you can't work?"

Economic status. Don't ask about an applicant's credit ratings, financial status, bankruptcy proceedings or past garnishments of wages. Instead of asking whether an applicant owns a car, ask: "Do you have a means of getting to work on time each day?"

Union or political affiliation. Don't ask.

Photograph. Never ask for a photograph before hiring.

ASK APPLICANTS THE SAME QUESTIONS

Failure to ask each applicant the same questions potentially can lead to hiring discrimination claims. Have a list of questions to ask all applicants.

DON'T MAKE EMPLOYMENT PROMISES

Promises made to job applicants may be interpreted by courts as implied employment contracts. Therefore, avoid statements like these:

1. You will have a long, rewarding and satisfying career ahead of you.
2. We will pay your moving expenses after one year of service.
3. You will be with us as long as you do your job.
4. You will not be fired without just cause.
5. This is a company where you can stay and grow.
6. In this company you'll have lots of job security.
7. Your salary will be $xxx annually. (Instead, quote salary on a weekly or monthly basis.)
8. There are no layoffs within this organization.

TAKE NOTES DURING THE INTERVIEW

Notes will help you in making a hiring decision. Your notes should contain the information listed below.

- On time or late for interview.
- Skills, knowledge, qualifications, training for the job.
- Specific experience in similar duties using similar skills.
- Potential to handle all aspects of the job.
- Reason for leaving prior employer.
- Reason(s) for gaps in employment record.
- Probability of success for job expansion—growth and promotion potential.
- General intelligence, alertness, comprehension.
- Ability to communicate orally—thoughts logically and clearly expressed (if applicable).
- Writing skills—evaluation of writing sample (if applicable).
- Desire demonstrated for the job—initiative and enthusiasm.
- Attitude toward work and dealing with others.
- Honesty and sincerity.
- Personal manner—confident, composed, nervous, etc.
- Personal feelings toward present and prior employers.
- Ability to do the essential job functions with or without reasonable accommodation.
- Hobbies, community activities—look for job-related qualities, such as leadership, responsibility, initiative.

Harassment/Improper Behavior

WHAT IS SEXUAL HARASSMENT?

Sexual harassment prohibited by law is unwelcome verbal or physical conduct of a sexual nature when:

1. submission to the conduct is made either an explicit or implicit term or condition of employment (such as promotion, training, timekeeping, overtime assignments, leaves of absence); *or*

2. submission to or rejection of the conduct is used as a basis for making employment decisions; *or*

3. the conduct has the purpose or effect of substantially interfering with an individual's work performance, or creating an intimidating, hostile, or offensive work environment.

IMPORTANT FACTS ABOUT SEXUAL HARASSMENT

- Sexual harassers may be coworkers, management personnel, or even non-employees (such as customers, sales representatives, or repair workers).

- Both men and women may be the victims of sexual harassment.

- Either a woman or a man may be the harasser.

- The parties to a sexual harassment lawsuit do not have to be of the opposite sex.

- The person who brings a sexual harassment lawsuit does not have to be the one at whom the sexual conduct was directed—it may be someone else who was affected by such conduct.

- Submission to the conduct does not necessarily mean the conduct was welcome.

OTHER TYPES OF ILLEGAL HARASSMENT

Sexual harassment is not the only type of harassment that is against the law. Harassment on the basis of race, religion, national origin, age, or disability is also illegal. Nonsexual harassment of an employee because of the employee's gender is unlawful as well.

Illegal "harassment" on the basis of race, color, religion, national origin, gender, disability, or age exists when:

1. an employee is subjected to verbal or physical conduct that shows hostility toward the employee because of the employee's race, color, religion, national origin, gender, disability, or age; *and*

2. the conduct has the purpose or effect of interfering with the employee's work performance or opportunities, or creating an intimidating, hostile or offensive work environment.

HARASSMENT EXAMPLES

- Offering or implying an employment-related reward (such as a promotion or raise) in exchange for sexual favors or submission to sexual conduct.

- Threatening or taking a negative employment action (such as termination, demotion, denial of a leave of absence) if sexual conduct is rejected.

- Unwelcome sexual advances or repeated flirtations.

- Unwelcome intentional touching of another person or other unwanted intentional physical contact (including patting, pinching, or brushing against another person's body).

- Unwelcome whistling, staring, or leering at another person.

- Asking unwelcome questions or making unwelcome comments about another person's sexual activities, dating, personal or intimate relationships, or appearance.

- Unwelcome sexually suggestive or flirtatious gifts.

- Unwelcome sexually suggestive or flirtatious letters, notes, e-mail, or voice mail.

- Conduct or remarks that are sexually suggestive or that demean or show hostility to a person because of the person's race, color, religion, national origin, gender, disability, or age (including jokes, pranks, teasing, obscenities, obscene or rude gestures or noises, slurs, epithets, taunts, negative stereotyping, threats, blocking of physical movement).

- Displaying or circulating pictures, objects, or written materials (including graffiti, cartoons, photographs, pinups, calendars, magazines, figurines, novelty items) that are sexually suggestive or that demean or show hostility to a person because of the person's race, color, religion, national origin, gender, disability, or age.

RUDE BEHAVIOR THAT DOESN'T QUALIFY AS HARASSMENT

Even if rude treatment of employees in the workplace does not meet the legal definitions of harassment, the conduct still should not be tolerated. Although not illegal under an employment statute, the conduct may be a common law tort, such as assault, battery, or intentional infliction of emotional distress. Depending on its severity, the conduct may even violate a criminal statute. Moreover, an employee who finds the conduct so intolerable that he or she quits may bring a constructive discharge lawsuit.

TAKE COMPLAINTS ABOUT IMPROPER BEHAVIOR SERIOUSLY

Even if the person who complains about alleged harassment or other rude conduct is a chronic complainer or if the behavior initially does not seem to be improper, take the complaint seriously. Further investigation may reveal that the conduct is unlawful or against company policy. Moreover, if the employee quits because he or she has come away with the impression that the company did not take the complaint seriously, the employer could face a constructive discharge lawsuit. Show the employee that the complaint is taken seriously by listening attentively and refraining from comments like "You're overreacting—I'm sure no harm was intended."

✓ CHECKLIST: HANDLING A COMPLAINT ABOUT MISCONDUCT

☐ Take the complaint seriously.

☐ Adopt a nonjudgmental, professional attitude toward the employee who brought the complaint.

☐ Thank the employee for bringing the complaint and provide assurance that no negative employee action will be taken again him or her for making the complaint.

☐ Assure the employee his or her complaint will be handled as discreetly and confidentially as possible.

☐ Ask for—but don't require—a written statement.

☐ Gather facts: get answers to who, what, when, where, why, and how; ask if there are any witnesses; ask if there is any documentation, such as letters, notes, e-mail messages, that may support the complaint; find out if the employee is afraid of retaliation from the persons who committed the alleged improper conduct.

☐ Ask what the employee wants to happen to resolve the problem, but don't promise the company will take that action.

☐ Tell the employee that there will be a prompt and thorough investigation and that appropriate remedial action will be taken if misconduct is found.

☐ Caution the employee of the risk of personal defamation liability if malicious or false statements are made during the investigation or if the matter is discussed with others.

☐ Carefully document all information gathered.

☐ Submit the information *immediately* and *confidentially* to the person designated by company policy to investigate harassment or other improper behavior.

WHAT IF NOBODY HAS COMPLAINED?

What if a supervisor has not received a complaint but suspects that harassment or other improper behavior is going on? Regardless of how the supervisor became aware of the suspected misconduct, the supervisor must *immediately* and *confidentially* notify the person designated by company policy to investigate improper behavior. Even if the suspected misconduct seems welcome or involves persons who work in another department, the supervisor still must report it.

Reporting the suspected misconduct will ensure that a thorough investigation will take place and that appropriate corrective action will be taken if the investigation confirms the supervisor's suspicions. By taking such action, legal problems can be avoided. On the other hand, failure of the supervisor to report the conduct can result in liability. For example, a company will be held liable for sexual harassment if a supervisor knew about the harassment but ignored it.

BE DISCREET

The privacy rights of both the accuser and accused must be respected at all times. Never discuss a complaint against an employee or information concerning the complaint with anyone who does not have a legitimate interest in and duty to receive the information. Ensure that all communications about the matter are strictly private and cannot be overheard. Never broadcast the results of an investigation as an example to others or as a training tool.

Workers with Disabilities/Injuries

WHO IS PROTECTED FROM DISABILITY BIAS?

The Americans with Disabilities Act (ADA) and other disability bias laws ban job discrimination on the basis of disability against any person who is a "qualified individual with a disability." Therefore, two requirements must be met before a person is protected from disability bias: (1) the person must have a disability; and (2) the person must be qualified for the job.

"Individual with a disability." A person has a disability if the person falls into *any* of the following three categories:

1. The person has a physical or mental impairment that substantially limits one or more of the person's major life activities. ("Major life activities" are activities that an average person can perform with little or no difficulty, such as hearing, seeing, speaking, breathing, performing manual tasks, walking, caring for oneself, learning or working.).

2. The person does not currently have such an impairment but has a record of a substantially limiting impairment.

3. The person has no such impairment but is regarded by management as having a substantially limiting impairment.

Qualification. An individual with a disability is "qualified" for a job if the person meets *both* of the following requirements:

1. The person meets the employer's job requirements for educational background, employment experience, skills, licenses and any other qualification standards that are related to the job; and.

2. The person can perform the essential functions of the job either with or without a reasonable accommodation of the person's disability. (Employers should carefully examine each job to determine which functions or tasks are essential to performance.).

Relationship with person with a disability. Persons who have a relationship or association with a person with a disability are also protected from discrimination on the basis of that relationship or association. This means that managers and supervisors are prohibited from making negative employment decisions based on unfounded concerns about the known disability of a family member or anyone else with whom the applicant or employee has a relationship or association. For example, it is illegal to refuse to hire a qualified applicant on the grounds that the applicant does volunteer work helping people with AIDS.

THE REASONABLE ACCOMMODATION DUTY

Employers have a duty to provide reasonable accommodations to the known physical or mental limitations of a qualified person with a disability. A reasonable accommodation is any change or adjustment to a job or work environment that permits a "qualified" applicant or employee with a disability to participate in the job application process, to perform the essential functions of a job, or to enjoy benefits and privileges of employment (such as access to meetings, lunchrooms, or social events) equal to those enjoyed by employees without disabilities.

Accommodation examples:

- Job restructuring
- Part-time or modified work schedules
- Leaves of absence
- Reassignment to a vacant position
- Acquiring or modifying equipment or devices
- Readers or interpreters
- Personal assistants
- Facility modifications
- Working from home
- Adjusting or modifying exams, training materials or policies

Notice of need for accommodation. Reasonable accommodations must be made only to the *known* physical or mental limitations of persons with disabilities. Generally, an accommodation request from an employee or applicant triggers the duty to accommodate. However, if an employee with a known disability is not performing well, a manager or supervisor may ask the employee if an accommodation is needed. When the appropriate accommodation is not readily apparent, the manager or supervisor must make a reasonable effort to identify one. The best way to do this is to consult informally with the applicant or employee about potential accommodations that would enable the individual to participate in the application process or perform the essential functions of the job. If the consultation does not identify an appropriate accommodation, the manager or supervisor may want to contact the US Equal Employment Opportunity Commission, state or local vocational rehabilitation agencies, or state or local organizations representing or providing services to individuals with disabilities. Another resource is the Job Accommodation Network (JAN). JAN is a free consultant service that helps employers make individualized accommodations. JAN's telephone number is 1-800-526-7234.

Undue hardship. Accommodations that would impose an undue hardship on the employer's business are not required. An "undue hardship" means that an accommodation would be unduly costly, extensive, substantial or disruptive, or would fundamentally alter the nature or operation of the employer's business. If a particular accommodation would be an undue hardship, the employer must: (1) try to identify another accommodation that will not pose such a hardship; and (2) consider whether funding for an accommodation is available from an outside source, such as a vocational rehabilitation agency, and if the cost of providing the accommodation can be offset by state or federal tax credits or deductions. The employer must also give the applicant or employee with a disability the opportunity to provide the accommodation or pay for the portion of the accommodation that constitutes an undue hardship.

Role of manager or supervisor. A manager or supervisor is responsible for arriving at an accommodation through give-and-take with the person who requests an accommodation. Accordingly, the manager or supervisor should promptly respond to an employee's request and develop appropriate time frames within which accommodations are provided. The manager or supervisor should also consider putting procedures for providing reasonable accommodations in writing (though this may not be necessary, particularly if you are a very small employer and have one person designated to receive and process accommodation requests.). However, the manager or supervisor should not try to determine whether a particular accommodation is an undue hardship for the company. Undue hardship decisions usually are made by upper management.

✓ CHECKLIST: FINDING A REASONABLE ACCOMMODATION

☐ Look at the particular job and determine its purpose and key functions.

☐ Consult with the person with a disability to find out the precise job-related limitations imposed by the person's disability.

☐ In consultation with the person, identify possible accommodations and assess how effective each accommodation would be in enabling the person to perform key job functions.

☐ If there are several possible accommodations, consider the person's preference and select the accommodation that best serves the needs of the person and the company.

☐ Notify the company official responsible for approving accommodations of: (1) the accommodation chosen; and (2) other accommodations to consider if that accommodation is rejected because of undue hardship.

PERIODIC MEDICAL EXAMS

After employment begins, an employer may make disability-related inquiries and require medical exams only if they are related to the job. In most instances, a need to make disability-related inquiries or require medical exams will be triggered by evidence of current performance problems or observable evidence that particular employees will pose a threat to themselves or others. If a manager or supervisor decides to fire or demote an employee with a disability based on the results of a medical exam, the manager or supervisor must demonstrate that the employee is unable to perform their essential job functions or, in fact, poses a threat that cannot be eliminated or reduced by a reasonable accommodation.

Managers and supervisors can always test for the current illegal use of drugs because that is not considered a medical exam under the ADA, but they may not generally subject employees to periodic alcohol testing. However, managers and supervisors may subject employees who have been in alcohol rehabilitation programs to periodic alcohol testing when the manager or supervisor has a reasonable belief that particular employees will pose a threat to themselves or others. Employers can always maintain and enforce rules prohibiting employees from being under the influence of alcohol in the workplace and may conduct alcohol testing for this purpose if there is a reasonable belief that an employee has been drinking during work hours.

CONFIDENTIALITY OF MEDICAL INFORMATION

With limited exceptions, managers and supervisors must keep any medical information learned about an applicant or employee confidential. Information can require confidentiality even if it contains no medical diagnosis or treatment course and even if it is not generated by a health care professional. For example, an employee's request for a reasonable accommodation would be considered confidential medical information. Managers and supervisors should not place medical information in regular personnel files. Rather, keep medical information in a separate files that is accessible only to designated officials. Medical information stored electronically must be similarly protected by storing it on a separate database.).

Sometimes medical information about applicants or employees has to be disclosed. Information that is otherwise confidential under the ADA may be disclosed: (1) to supervisors and managers where they need the information in order to provide a reasonable accommodation or to meet an employee's work restrictions; (2) to first aid and safety personnel if an employee would need emergency treatment or require some other assistance (such as help during an emergency evacuation) because of a medical condition; (3) to individuals investigating compliance with the ADA and other disability bias laws; and (4) pursuant to workers' compensation laws for insurance purposes.

RIGHTS OF PERSONS INJURED ON THE JOB

Employees who are injured on the job or who become disabled due to an on-the-job injury or illness are entitled to benefits required by state workers' compensation laws. Workers' compensation laws usually provide for reimbursement of medical costs and wage-loss benefits. If a person's work-related illness is a "serious health condition" under the Family and Medical Leave Act (FMLA), the person will also be entitled to the Act's leave-of-absence and return-to-work rights. Moreover, if the person meets the ADA's definition of "qualified individual with a disability," the person will have job accommodation rights too. Leave-of-absence rights under the FMLA and ADA are discussed in the next chapter.

TREAT EVERY INJURY AS LEGITIMATE

The manager or supervisor is usually the first person on the scene of an injury. Respond immediately to injured workers and create a supportive environment for them. Treat *every* injury as legitimate, even if there are suspicious circumstances. Injured workers who are not treated seriously may file a lawsuit.

✓ CHECKLIST: WHAT TO DO WHEN A WORKER IS INJURED

☐ Immediately administer first aid.

☐ Accompany the injured worker to a selected medical provider.

☐ Report incident within company.

☐ Notify the worker's family.

☐ Report to claim handler outside company (insurance company or third-party administrator) if required to do so under company policy.

☐ Determine whether the injury is covered by workers' compensation.

☐ Contact union, if applicable.

☐ If the employee misses work because of the injury, determine whether the injury is a "serious health condition" under the FMLA. If the injury is determined to be a serious health condition, notify the employee within two business days of such determination that the leave is designated as FMLA leave.

☐ Follow up with the employee and/or family.

☐ Develop return-to-work plan.

☐ Forward mail.

☐ Use a "wellness" approach (cards, phone calls, visits) to continue to reinforce company's concern.

☐ Update return-to-work plan.

☐ Refer for pain management evaluation of chronic pain, if appropriate.

☐ Maintain contact with the injured employee and/or the family.

✓ CHECKLIST: DATA TO GATHER FOR EACH INJURY

As the manager or supervisor of someone who has suffered a work-related injury or illness, you will need to have certain kinds of information available. You will be communicating with the injured worker and the family, with the treating physician, with the in-house benefits or claims department, and possibly with the insurance company. Following is a list of information that you will need to know to make the job go smoothly:

ABOUT THE EMPLOYEE

☐ Name
☐ Address
☐ Phone
☐ Social Security number
☐ Sex
☐ Date of birth
☐ Marital status
☐ Dependents
☐ State hired
☐ Date of hire
☐ Job classification (insurance class or company classification)

ABOUT THE INJURY

☐ Date of injury
☐ Date of death (if applicable)
☐ State of injury
☐ Nature of injury (sprain, fracture, etc.)
☐ Body part(s) affected
☐ Source of injury (machines, hand tools, buildings, etc.)
☐ Type of injury (fall, struck by, overexertion, repetitive motion trauma)
☐ Witnesses
☐ Work process involved (i.e. lifting, carrying, etc.)
☐ Industry
☐ Division
☐ Plant or location
☐ Department
☐ Supervisor
☐ Job
☐ Time of day
☐ Shift

ABOUT THE CLAIM

- ☐ Date employer first notified
- ☐ Who was notified? By whom?
- ☐ Date employer's workers' compensation claims department notified
- ☐ Other benefits lost (Did the company stop paying vacation, health benefits, etc.?)
- ☐ Other benefits received
- ☐ Date of first payment
- ☐ Projected return-to-work date
- ☐ Date case closed
- ☐ Lost days
- ☐ Total benefits paid
- ☐ Vocational rehabilitation activity

Time Off from Work

FAMILY AND MEDICAL LEAVE

Types of leave. The Family and Medical Leave Act (FMLA) guarantees an employee up to 12 weeks of job-protected leave each year for any one or more of the following reasons:

- birth of child
- adoption of child
- foster care of child
- child's serious health condition
- spouse's serious health condition
- parent's serious health condition
- employee's serious health condition
- employee's pregnancy

Maternity and paternity leave. FMLA leave for the birth, adoption, or foster care of a child can be taken by men and women. Denying leave to an eligible employee on the basis of gender can result in FMLA *and* sex discrimination liability.

"Serious health condition." A "serious health condition" is an illness, injury, or impairment that involves any of the following:

- Any period of incapacity connected with inpatient care (overnight stay) in a hospital, hospice, or residential medical care facility.
- Any period of incapacity requiring absence of more than three days from work, school, or other regular daily activities that also involves continuing treatment by or under the supervision of a health care provider.
- Continuing treatment by or under the supervision of a health care provider for a chronic or long-term health condition that is incurable or is so serious that, if not treated, would likely result in a period of incapacity for more than three days.
- Incapacity due to pregnancy or prenatal care.

Examples of serious health conditions:

- heart attacks
- heart conditions requiring bypass surgery
- strokes
- most types of cancer
- back conditions requiring extensive therapy or surgery
- severe respiratory conditions
- pneumonia
- emphysema
- asthma
- severe arthritis
- severe nervous disorders
- injuries caused by serious accidents (on or off the job)

- pregnancy

- miscarriage

- complications related to pregnancy (for example, severe morning sickness)

- childbirth

- recovery from childbirth

- long-term chronic conditions (such as Alzheimer's or other diseases in terminal stage)

  - kidney disease

  - diabetes

  - epilepsy

  - migraines

  - appendicitis

Nonserious health conditions. Unless complications develop, the following conditions generally are not serious health conditions: the common cold, flu, ear aches, upset stomach, minor ulcers, headaches other than migraines, routine dental or orthodontia problems, or periodontal disease. Cosmetic treatments are serious health conditions only if inpatient care is required or complications develop. FMLA leave in connection with substance abuse may only be taken for treatment of substance abuse.

Employee eligibility. To be eligible for FMLA leave, an employee must have worked for the company at least 12 months before the start of leave (the 12 months do not have to be continuous), and the employee must have worked 1,250 hours during that time. Managers or supervisors who are unsure whether an employee meets these requirements should notify their Human Resources department.

Employee notice of leave. When possible, employees must give 30 days' advance notice of their intent to take leave. If 30-day advance notice is impractical, as in case of medical emergency, notice must be given as soon as possible (usually within one or two business days after the employee learns of the need to take leave).

In giving notice, employees do not have to specifically state that they are taking FMLA leave. Rather, it is the responsibility of the individual who oversees FMLA matters for the employer to determine whether the leave qualifies as FMLA leave based on information received directly from the employee (or the employee's spokesperson, like a family member, if the employee is incapacitated).

Designation of FMLA leave. Whoever oversees FMLA matters for the employer must act quickly in deciding whether leave qualifies as FMLA leave. Once enough information is acquired to know that leave qualifies as FMLA, the employee must be told within two business days—either orally or in writing—that the leave is designated as FMLA leave. If the notice is oral, written notice must be given no later than the next payroll period.

Medical certification. Companies can require certification of a serious health condition by a health care provider. Certification can also be required to confirm fitness to return to work. An employee must be given written notice of a requirement for medical certification in support of a leave request. Requests for certification should be made at the time an employee asks for leave or within two business days after.

Pay. FMLA leave is unpaid. However, both the employer and the employee have the option to substitute paid leave they have already earned (such as vacation or sick leave) during FMLA leave. If substitution of paid leave is required, notification to the employee must be made within two business days of the employee's notice of the need for leave, or when a determination is made that the leave is FMLA-qualifying. The designation must be made before the leave starts, unless there is insufficient information about the employee's reason for taking leave.

Notice of intent to return to work. Managers and supervisors have the right to require employees on FMLA to report periodically regarding their status and their intent to return to work once their leave expires. Requests for status reports must be reasonable under the particular circumstances of the employee's case.

FMLA protections end for employees who say they are definitely not returning to work. Be careful: the law requires that an employee's intention not to return to work be absolutely clear, certain, and subject to no possible misunderstanding. An employee's statement that "I don't think I'll be able to come back to work, but I'll sure try" would thus not be definite notice.

Job restoration. Upon returning from FMLA leave, an employee must be restored to his or her original job, or to a job with equivalent pay, benefits, and working conditions. The employee cannot be forced to return early into a "light duty" job.

AVOID DISABILITY BIAS PITFALLS

Leave as accommodation. If an employee who requests medically-related time off from work is not entitled to FMLA leave, workers' compensation leave, or leave under company policy, do not automatically deny leave. Consider whether the person is a "qualified individual with a disability" under the Americans with Disabilities Act (ADA) for whom the requested absence may be a reasonable accommodation.

Extension of leave. If an employee's medically-related absence continues beyond the amount of leave permitted under the FMLA, workers' compensation, or company policy, do not automatically take disciplinary action. Consider whether the person is a "qualified individual with a disability" for whom extension of leave may be a reasonable accommodation.

Reinstatement after accommodation leave. If a qualified employee with a disability is provided leave as a reasonable accommodation, the employee must be placed in the *same* job upon returning to work, unless doing so would impose an undue hardship on the company.

Accommodation upon return. If an employee is unable to perform his or her former job after returning from a medically-related absence, do not automatically demote or terminate the employee. Consider whether the person is a "qualified individual with a disability" who can be reasonably accommodated to perform that job. If accommodation is not possible in the employee's former job, determine whether a vacant, equivalent position is available that the employee can perform, with or without reasonable accommodation.

Confidentiality of medical information. Medical information relating to employees or their family members must be kept in separate, confidential files. Special rules for medical records are noted in the chapter titled "References/Defamation/Privacy."

MILITARY LEAVE

Employee eligibility. The Uniformed Services Employment and Reemployment Rights Act (USERRA) requires that an employee be granted leave for military service if the following two criteria are met:

1. The employee or an appropriate military officer provides advance oral or written notice of military service. (USERRA does not require any specific time for giving advance notice.) However, no notice is required if doing so is impossible or unreasonable due to military necessity or other reasons.

2. The combined length of the employee's prior military absences from the company does not exceed five years (see "Duration of service," below).

Reasonableness of leave request. An eligible employee's leave request must be granted. Even if a manager or supervisor finds the timing, duration, frequency, or nature of an eligible employee's military service to be unreasonable, the employee cannot be denied leave from work.

Types of military service. Military service for which leave may be taken includes not just absences for active duty, but also absences for training, weekend drills, summer camp, funeral honors duty, fitness-for-duty examinations, and volunteer service as a member of the National Disaster Medical System.

Duration of leave. USERRA places a five-year limit on the *combined* length of an employee's military service absences from an employer. However, some types of service, including annual summer training and monthly weekend drills required for reservists and National Guard members, are exempt from the five-year limit. Ask your Human Resources department to do the five-year calculation, which can be quite tricky.

Pay. USERRA does not require pay during military leave. However, some companies voluntarily pay reservists the difference between their regular wage and the military pay received during annual summer training.

Employees on military leave have the right to use any accrued vacation or similar leave with pay during military service. However, it is against the law to require an employee to do so.

Notice of return. If an employee's military service is 31 or fewer days, the employee must, barring excusable circumstances, report to work by the beginning of the first regularly scheduled work day that falls eight hours after the employee returns home. If the employee's service is 31 to 180 days, the employee must, barring excusable circumstances, submit an application for reemployment within 14 days after completing military service. The employee must submit an application for reemployment within 90 after completing military service if the employee's service was 181 or more days. "Applications" for reemployment can be written or oral.

Reemployment rights are not automatically lost if an employee fails to meet these limits. Rather, the employee will then be subject to the company's rules governing unexcused absences.

Reemployment eligibility. Generally, a person must be promptly rehired (usually within two weeks of the date the service membver applies for reemployment, absent unusual circumstances) after military service if the person provided advance oral or written notice (unless doing so would have been impossible or unreasonable); the person did not exceed the five-years service limit; and the person timely reported to work or applied for reemployment. If a person's reemployment eligibility is in doubt, the matter should immediately be referred to the Human Resources department.

Notice of intent not to return to work. Resigning from a job in order to enter military service does not cut off a person's reemployment rights. As long as the person meets the eligibility requirements, the person must be reemployed. The person may lose entitlement to certain job benefits *during* military service if the person voluntarily gives written notice of an intent not to return to work after military service. But such a notice will not deprive the person of reemployment rights and benefits when the person returns from military service.

Reinstatement after leave. Generally, a person returning from military service must be placed in the job the person would have held if the person remained continuously employed, or, if the person is unqualified or cannot become qualified for that job, in the person's preservice job. If the person cannot be trained to perform either of those jobs, the person must be placed in any other job that the person can perform. Reasonable accommodations must be provided to persons with service-connected disabilities.

OTHER LEAVES REQUIRED BY LAW

Jury duty leave. Federal law gives employees the right to take time off to serve as jurors in federal courts. State laws give employees the right to serve on state and local juries.

Witness duty leave. A number of states have laws permitting employees to serve as witnesses in court.

Time off to vote. State laws generally allow employees at least two hours of time off to vote.

Time off for school functions. Several states have laws requiring employers to give employees time off to attend certain functions at their children's schools.

Bone marrow or organ donation. Some states require employers to grant employee requests for time off to donate bone marrow or organs.

COMPANY-OFFERED LEAVES

Companies often make available to employees various types of leave that are not required by law. These may include:

- Vacations
- Scheduled holidays
- "Floating" personal holidays
- Bereavement leave
- Marriage leave
- Educational leave
- Sabbaticals
- Sick leave
- Short-term disability leave
- Long-term disability leave

Moreover, some companies may "add on" to a leave-of-absence statute by providing for even more rights than the law requires. For example, company policy may allow a longer period of family and medical leave than is required by statute. Or, a company may voluntarily choose to pay employees for certain military-related absences.

BE FAMILIAR WITH COMPANY POLICY

Managers and supervisors must know and follow their company's leave-of-absence policies. Failure to observe employees' rights under company policy can result in lawsuits. Specifically, managers and supervisors should at least know:

- The types of leave available under company policy.
- Leave documentation requirements.
- Which types of leave accrue and carry over into the next year.
- Who is eligible for each type of leave.
- Whether proof of a need to take leave is required.
- Employee notice requirements: When must notice of a need to take leave be given? Who must be notified? Must the notice be in writing?
- Company notice requirements: What kinds of notice must be given to employees for each type of leave? When must notice be given? Who is responsible for giving notice?
- How much leave may be taken.
- Whether pay will continue during leave.
- Types of leave that run concurrently.
- Impact on seniority.
- The position to which a returning employee is entitled.
- Consequences of failure to return to work on time.

Drug and Alcohol Problems

WHO IS PROTECTED?

Alcoholics. Alcoholics are protected from discrimination by the Americans with Disabilities Act (ADA) and other disability bias laws. However, an alcoholic can be disciplined if the person's alcohol use affects the person's job performance or conduct to the point that the person is not qualified for the job. Such discipline must be based on the person's poor performance or conduct, not the person's alcoholism. Furthermore, the discipline cannot be harsher than that imposed on other employees for the same performance or conduct.

> *Example::* An alcoholic is late to work. The employee can be disciplined for tardiness, even if alcohol use caused the employee's lateness. But the employee cannot be more severely disciplined than other employees who are tardy.

Illegal drug users. Current users of illegal drugs are not protected by the ADA. Consequently, employees can be disciplined or fired for current use of illegal drugs. However, an illegal drug user who also has a disability, such as epilepsy, is still protected from discrimination on the basis of that disability. "Illegal drugs" do not include drugs prescribed by a doctor or other licensed health care professional. "Current" illegal drug use means that the illegal use of drugs is occurring or has occurred recently enough to indicate that an employee's involvement with drugs is an ongoing problem.

Former drug addicts. The ADA protects rehabilitated drug addicts who no longer use illegal drugs. Recovering drug addicts who are participating in a drug treatment program and who have stopped using illegal drugs are also protected.

> *Example::* An employee is involved in an accident that damages equipment. If a drug test indicates recent cocaine use, the employee can be disciplined for illegal drug use. But if the test shows no recent illegal drug use and the employee is currently participating in a drug treatment program, disciplining the employee may violate the ADA if other employees who had similar accidents in the past were not disciplined.

Persons mistakenly thought to be addicts. Never discipline or fire someone for illegal drug use in the absence of solid evidence that the person really is using illegal drugs. Disciplining or firing an employee on the basis of a mistaken belief that the employee is addicted to illegal drugs may result in liability under the ADA. Liability for defamation could also result.

Medical use of marijuana. In the late 1990s states began passing laws legalizing the use of marijuana for medical purposes. The majority of these laws specifically do not require employers to accommodate the medical use of marijuana or to pay for it under their health insurance programs. When state laws don't exclude an employer's obligation to accommodate a disability, the argument could be made that accommodation is required because the medical use of marijuana is legal. However, in June 2005, the U.S. Supreme Court settled the question of legality by ruling that the federal government can prosecute individuals for personal medical use of marijuana, even if the use is in compliance with state law. The decision allows employers with drug-testing programs to rely on the fact that, under federal law, possession and use of marijuana is illegal regardless of its purpose, even if it will not be prosecuted at the state level. Nevertheless, managers and supervisor should guard against discriminating on the basis of an individual's status as a medical marijuana user.

Leave for treatment. FMLA leave is available for treatment for substance abuse, provided that the employee has met the definition of having a serious health condition. However, absence because of an employee's use of a substance, rather than for treatment, does not qualify for FMLA leave. Treatment for substance abuse does not prevent an employer from taking employment action against an employee, if the employee has an established policy that is applied in a non-discriminatory manner and has been communicated to all employees. An employee may be terminated, pursuant to that policy, whether or not the employee is presently taking FMLA leave.

SHOULD THE EMPLOYEE BE PUNISHED OR REHABILITATED?

If alcohol or drug use has caused an employee to have a dangerous accident, endanger another employee or not show up for work frequently, it may be tempting to simply fire or suspend the employee. However, supervisors should keep in mind that the person may be protected by the ADA. And, from a bottom-line viewpoint—if the employee was once a productive member of the company—it may be in the company's best interest to give rehabilitation a chance rather than fire the person. Otherwise, the company may lose time and money in selecting and training a replacement who does not perform at the level this employee once performed.

It is also tempting to simply ignore the problem by letting the employee get by with mistakes or absences. One study indicates that substance abusers in the private sector are protected by supervisors for an average of *eight years*. Instead of covering up for problems, the supervisor should let the employee collect the natural consequences of his or her actions. If a sick day normally requires a doctor's note, insist on a doctor's note. If a slowdown in production would normally mean a warning, give the appropriate warning.

Rehabilitation *is* possible—the supervisor does not need to give up on the person. Experts say that although people with substance abuse problems will endure the loss of their driver's license and even their marriage or family, they often are shocked into accepting help when faced with losing their job.

HOW TO CONFRONT AN EMPLOYEE

First-level supervisors will be the first to observe signs of a substance abuse problem that affects a person's job. Increased absenteeism, long lunches, a decrease in work quality or quantity, frequent trips to the restroom, sloppy appearance, on-the-job injuries and difficulty in following instructions or recalling things are signs that may indicate a substance abuse problem. Experts say that the supervisor should confront the employee about the job performance problem with a caring but firm attitude. Here are some basics about confronting the employee:

• Let the employee know that you are concerned about the slipping job performance and are there to help.

• Don't try to diagnose the employee's problem—that is not your area of expertise. Base the discussion on the decrease in job performance, not on the suspected alcoholism or drug abuse, unless there is objective, verifiable proof that abuse is the root of the problem.

• Make expectations clear by communicating acceptable levels of job perform-ance and pointing out where the employee falls short. Be prepared to show the employee records that objectively indicate performance mistakes, absenteeism or other problems.

• Clarify that the company does not want to lose the employee's services and expertise, but that it will not tolerate the decline in performance. Set time limits for improvement.

• If it is determined that the employee does have an alcohol or drug abuse problem, job performance is not likely to improve unless the employee gets help for the problem. Offer the employee help through the company's Employee Assistance Program or refer the employee to social services agencies.

• Be firm in encouraging the employee to seek assistance before any absenteeism or performance problems get worse and job loss becomes a possibility. Let the employee know that he or she is the only one who can agree to accept help.

• Don't create hostility by being judgmental. Say "this behavior can cost you your job," rather than "you are wrong" or "you should know better."

• Don't ask why the employee does things—that only gives the employee the chance to make excuses and tell sympathy-evoking stories. The excuse or story doesn't matter—the employee is always responsible for his or her behavior and job performance.

• Don't make idle disciplinary threats. Establish specific check-back dates and follow through with warnings if performance doesn't improve.

PROVIDE RIDES HOME FOR INTOXICATED EMPLOYEES

An employee returns to work after lunch intoxicated. The employee clearly is unable to work. Is it proper for the supervisor to order the employee to clock out and leave the premises?

An employer who clocks out and sends home an impaired employee invites legal problems. The supervisor is exercising control over the situation. The employee is being told to leave the premises, which often is by car. If the employee later gets in an accident, the employer can be sued for negligently allowing an impaired person to operate a motor vehicle. The better handling of the situation would be to require the employee to take a cab home or arrange for some other form of transportation. That may invite hard feelings, but there will be no legal problem.

Union Activities

WORKERS' PROTECTED LABOR RIGHTS

The National Labor Relations Act (NLRA) gives employees four basic rights:

1. The right to join or form a union.

2. The right to bargain collectively, through employee-chosen representatives, about wages, hours, and working conditions.

3. The right for employees to act together to improve their working conditions, whether or not they are unionized.

4. The right to refrain from taking part in labor activities.

PROHIBITED LABOR PRACTICES

Managers and supervisors should be aware of the following broad categories of "unfair labor practices" that the NLRA prohibits:

- Interfering with, restraining, or coercing employees who are exercising their protected labor rights.

- Dominating or interfering with the formation of a union, or contributing financial or other support to a union.

- Discriminating against employees or applicants on the basis of union membership.

- Refusing to bargain with a union that represents a majority of employees.

- Entering into an agreement with a union to not do business with another company.

UNION REPRESENTATION AT INVESTIGATORY INTERVIEWS

If an employee in a unionized workplace requests that a union representative be present at an interview with a manager or supervisor, the request should not automatically be refused. The employee has a right to bring a union representative if the interview is part of an investigation and may result in the employee being disciplined or fired.

If the purpose of the interview is to inform the employee about a final disciplinary decision that already has been made, or if the employee did not ask for representation, the employee does not have a right to have a representative present.

When an employee in a unionized workplace requests union representation at an investigatory interview, the employee's request can be denied. The employee then has the choice of being interviewed without a union representative or not being interviewed at all. However, it is illegal to go ahead with the interview without a union representative if the employee makes neither choice and still wants a union representative there.

TIPS FOR AVOIDING LIABILITY DURING UNION CAMPAIGNS

- Don't fire or take other negative action against employees for participating in union activity.

- Avoid assigning union supporters to unpleasant or non-routine tasks.

- Don't tell employees that they will be fired or that anything else negative will occur for participating in union activities.

- Don't visit employees in their homes to discuss a union.

- Don't promise or grant benefits to employees in order to dissuade them from voting for a union.

- Don't ask employees or applicants questions about their union sympathies, activities, or knowledge of union affairs.

- Don't attend union meetings, spy on union organizing activities, or in any other way appear to be watching organizing activity.

- Don't prohibit employees from soliciting union membership or distributing union literature during meal periods, breaks, or other nonworking time.

- Don't stop employees from carrying union cards, displaying union buttons, or wearing T-shirts that bear union legends supporting a union (unless those actions interfere with work activity or the company prohibits similar nonunion propaganda to be worn or displayed).

- Don't take union literature from employees.

- Don't take part in any activity that is a direct rejection of a union, such as a petition to reject the union.

- Don't financially support a union.

- Don't try to influence employees' choice of a union.

NONUNION ACTIVITY CAN BE PROTECTED

Unlike their union counterparts, employees in nonunionized workplaces do not have a right to have a coworker present duirng an investigatory interview that may result in discipline. However, the right of employees to act together for their mutual aid and protection applies not just to unionized employees, but also to employees who work in nonunionized workplaces. This right is explained in the next chapter.

Whistleblowing/Group Complaints

WHAT IS WHISTLEBLOWER PROTECTION?

Discharged employees often claim that they were fired because they "blew the whistle" on their employer. That is, they reported something that the employer did that may violate the law or a clear public policy. The most common successful claims involve complaints about safety, environmental hazards or fraudulent practices.

Whistleblowing does not always involve big, eventful disclosures—it can arise from situations as simple as an employee making a complaint about another employee's actions or refusing to do something that the employee feels is illegal. Sometimes the complaint may have seemed insignificant to the supervisor and unrelated to the termination. Consequently, in every termination, the supervisor should examine whether the employee may feel like he or she has been fired for making complaints or for reporting any wrongdoing.

Most states have enacted laws to protect employees who are whistleblowers. Even if a state does not have a statute giving whistleblower protection, the state may allow common law violation-of-public-policy lawsuits. Some state courts have ruled that it violates public policy to fire someone for disclosing a practice that could harm the public or violate the law.

There is also a federal law that gives federal employees whistleblower protection for disclosures of waste or fraud. Another federal law gives whistleblower protection to employees of publicly traded companies who provide information to governmental authorities about conduct they believe to be mail, wire, securities or shareholder fraud.Moreover, the federal employment laws discussed in this book contain anti-retaliation provisions that prohibit firing or disciplining an employee for filing a complaint or for testifying or exercising other rights under those laws.

WHO ARE PROTECTED WHISTLEBLOWERS?

Coverage under state laws varies. Some laws require an employee to complain to company officials to give the company a chance to correct the problem before going "public." Other laws only protect people who report alleged misconduct to the public officials who have authority to investigate the allegations. The complaint does not always have to be valid—some courts will require only a reasonable belief that the company was doing something wrong. If an employee makes a claim that his or her discharge is a public policy violation, the exact circumstances under which the employee will qualify for whistleblower protection are even more vague. Generally, the court will examine whether the employee made the disclosures in good faith, rather than maliciously, and whether the alleged wrongdoing is a violation or a danger that people clearly should not be fired for reporting.

WHISTLEBLOWING EXAMPLES

Example 1:: An insurance company employee reported to senior management that serious deficiencies and irregularities in the company's claims department amounted to violation of a state law on unfair insurance claim settlements. The employee was fired shortly afterward. A court ruled that the employee was wrongfully discharged in violation of public policy.

Example 2:: A financial officer was fired after he told his superiors that the company's accounting practices may violate federal securities law by overvaluing certain assets. The employee's wrongful discharge claim was valid, even though he voiced the objection only to superiors rather than to regulatory authorities. He did not have to show that the accounting practices were definitely a violation of securities laws—only that he reasonably believed the practices to be illegal.

Example 3:: A gas station attendant claimed that he was fired for refusing to pump leaded gas into a car requiring unleaded fuel. Federal laws designed to ensure clean air showed a clear public policy against firing someone for such an action. If the employee could prove that his refusal to commit an illegal act was the reason for his discharge, he would have a valid wrongful discharge claim, a court ruled.

PROTECTED GROUP COMPLAINTS

The National Labor Relations Act, in addition to giving all employees, whether they are unionized or not, the right to form unions and to bargain, also gives employees the right to engage in other activities for their mutual aid and protection. Just as employers cannot fire or discipline someone for union activities, they cannot fire or discipline employees for these other "protected concerted activities." An employee does not have to belong to a union or be in a union shop to be protected. How do you know when an action that an employee takes is protected concerted activity?

1. The activity must be "concerted."— First, the employee must be acting "in concert" with other employees. The clearest form of concerted activity is when two or more employees as a group bring a common complaint. For instance, three employees may refuse to do any more work until the boss raises their pay. This is protected concerted activity for which they cannot be disciplined. However, they can be treated as economic strikers and be permanently replaced by other workers.

A more difficult call is when a single employee brings a complaint to a manager. If the complaint is strictly about the employee's *own personal* working conditions, pay or safety, it is not concerted activity. But the activity may be concerted if the employee acts alone to raise concerns about working conditions that affect other employees, or if several employees select one employee as a spokesperson to voice a complaint. However, simply getting other employees to join in on one employee's personal complaint does not make the activity concerted.

The basic point for supervisors and managers to remember is that if two or more people come forward with a complaint or suggestion, there is a labor law issue. Also, if one person comes forward to make a general complaint or suggestion about working conditions affecting several employees, that employee may also have protections under labor law.

2. The activity must be "protected."— The employee's action must also be "protected." The complaint must be about working conditions that affect employees on the job. This may include wages, benefits, hours or plant and equipment conditions. A complaint about doing business in China, for example, would not be protected since it is presumably unrelated to employees' jobs. A complaint about a supervisor's philosophy and managerial policies is not protected if it does not relate to employees' jobs or working conditions.

Some undesirable activities are not protected even if they are job-related. For instance, work slowdowns are not a protected activity. Employees can apply pressure to their employer by stopping work altogether and refusing pay—a strike—but they cannot lawfully accept pay without giving the company a full day of work in return. Similarly, a refusal to perform part of a job—say, overtime work—is an unprotected, recurrent work stoppage. Courts view this as employees merely trying to set their own terms of employment.

Employees who get carried away with actions that are malicious, defamatory, or insubordinate are also not engaging in "protected" activity. However, not every derogatory, loud, or obscene workplace comment will qualify as malicious. If the comments or actions are connected with a legitimate dispute and are not accompanied by threatening gestures, the activity is more likely to be "protected."

GROUP COMPLAINT EXAMPLES

Example 1:: Several mechanics gathered in a break area and refused to clock in and go to work until the company president would agree to meet with them to discuss wages. They left after a few hours, in response to a message from the president telling them that they could either go to work, leave the premises, or stay and be fired. The employees were fired a few days later. These discharges were unlawful because the attempt to meet with management was a peaceful, protected work stoppage. By staying in the break area, the mechanics made sure they did not interfere with the employer's business or other employees. An employer can refuse to pay employees who engage in a work stoppage—and it can even put them on inactive status and hire replacement workers—but it cannot discipline them.

Example 2:: A group of employees put their grievances about wages and working conditions in writing and went to see their supervisor. Unsatisfied with the results of their meetings with management, they arranged a "sick-out" in protest of the unresolved grievances, with everyone calling in sick on the same day (which is legally a protected strike). In response, the employer required the employees to present a doctor's certificate before they could return to work. The company's action was unlawful since the company didn't usually require doctors' certificates for one-day absences.

Example 3:: Because of a dispute about overtime wages, a group of employees announced that they would not work overtime hours. They left at the end of their regular hours. The employer lawfully fired them. Their refusal to work overtime was not a protected activity since it was a recurrent partial withholding of work aimed at setting the terms of their own work.

Performance Appraisals

Why conduct performance appraisals?

What are the goals of the organization? Where is it trying to go? Effective performance appraisal requires goals. In an organization where there are no clear goals or employees are not appraised about their performance relative to those goals, there is often a collective lack of focus that can cost a company market share and bottom-line profit.

Goals must be established for the organization as a whole. The basic purpose of performance appraisal is to direct and improve an employee's performance relative to company goals. Performance appraisals are a tool supervisors can use to manage towards organization goals. When done correctly, performance appraisals achieve two important purposes:

1. **Improve employee performance.** Good performance appraisal involves setting goals for employees to meet and then providing regular feedback on how employees are doing in meeting those goals.

2. **Create a record of performance.** The appraisal process should create a written record of performance, both acceptable and unacceptable. Written performance appraisals provide a legitimate basis for making personnel decisions. If an employee must be fired, effective performance appraisals are often the most persuasive proof that an employee was justifiably terminated.

What are the elements of good performance appraisals?

Remember two basic rules for effective performance appraisals:

1. Descriptions of employee performance must be based on factors relevant to the job.

2. Performance must be described in specific, objective terms, measured in terms of behavior or actions on the job that can be observed. Avoid subjective, vague or overly broad descriptions such as "poor attitude" or "no initiative."

Compare the following examples of subjective, vague descriptions of behavior with the more objective and specific descriptions of on-the-job activity.

Subjective	Objective
Lacks customer orientation.	Does not greet customers within defined timeframe.
Chronically absent.	Absent 6 workdays in last month.
Does not care about quality.	Has error rate of 10%.
Lacks interest in work.	Does not complete assignments on deadline.

Performance appraisals must be accurate

Performance appraisal records are one of the first things lawyers will look at when investigating a termination. Appraisals that do not accurately reflect a record of poor performance can be used against an employer. For instance, appraisals that do not identify performance problems can be used to refute a supervisor's contention that an employee was fired for poor performance.

Accurate appraisals verify the performance reasons why an employee was disciplined or discharged. If an employee claims that he was unlawfully fired because of his age or race, for example, effective performance appraisals can show that the employee was fired solely because of his poor job performance.

The following examples show how accurate performance appraisals can help companies defend against lawsuits alleging that a termination was unlawful:

Example 1:: After 60-year-old employee is laid off, he files a lawsuit claiming that he was unlawfully chosen for termination because of his age. But the employer uses past performance ratings to show that the employee was one of the three lowest performers chosen for layoff. Performance ratings stating that the employee needed to improve his work provided a legitimate business reason for the discharge, agreed the court hearing the dispute.

Example 2:: A 53-year-old manufacturing manager files a lawsuit alleging that he was fired because of his age. He argues that his plant's production performance was excellent in the past; any recent decline in production is due to general economic conditions, he says. The employer shows, however, that the decision to fire was based on the manager's inability to get along with people. Evaluation records show that the manager had been repeatedly warned about his inability to communicate effectively with superiors and subordinates. The court found that those appraisals showed that the manager was not performing up to expectations.

Example 3:: A sales representative claims he was fired due to his race. According to company performance appraisal records, however, the employee did not respond to a performance improvement program that identified specific deficiencies in performance and set out specific goals for improvement. These goals included objective descriptions of improved selling technique, including the elimination of customer complaints, better organization and planning, and utilization of more sophisticated sales techniques. The company's defense was successful.

✓ Checklist: Preparing for the appraisal meeting

☐ **Know the employee's job functions.** Decide which functions are the most critical. Define the specific activities and responsibilities that contribute to those functions.

☐ **Gather information.** Compare the employee's actual performance to performance standards. Use notes, production reports, customer and coworker feedback, and any other available records to back up your appraisal. Ask the employee to provide a self-assessment.

☐ **Identify critical incidents.** Identify situations where the employee has made an outstanding contribution or has fallen short when attempting to fulfill an important job function.

☐ **Review previous appraisals.** Determine whether the employee has met realistic performance goals set in previous reviews.

☐ **Prepare a development plan.** The plan should aim to strengthen conduct that leads to good performance and to change conduct that pulls performance down.

☐ **Plan for the appraisal discussion.** Limit the discussion to only those elements of performance that are critical, very important, or important. Also allow time to discuss the employee's self-assessment and to explore the causes of any problems, as well as time to set goals and work out a development plan for the next review period.

☐ **Choose a time and place for the meeting.** Plan enough time for the meeting. Make sure the meeting does not conflict with either your schedule or the employee's. Give the employee enough advance notice to prepare psychologically for the meeting. Choose a private place for the meeting where you and the employee will not be interrrupted.

Avoid the temptation to "soften" a negative appraisal

Performance appraisals must be an accurate reflection of what an employee actually did on the job. Be realistic in your assessment; don't sugarcoat a negative performance appraisal. Softening a negative performance appraisal can result in the employee failing to understand that he or she is doing a poor job.

Remember that negative appraisals are not designed to punish people. Rather, effective negative feedback is intended to notify an employee of behavior that falls below expectations and provide an opportunity to improve that behavior before more serious discipline is imposed.

Tips for making negative appraisals positive

- View the appraisal meeting not as a punishment, but as a positive tool for helping the employee to improve.

- Be familiar with the details of the employee's job, workload, working conditions, and resources available.

- Be prepared to describe performance deficiencies objectively, specifically, and honestly.

- Keep a positive tone. Don't point fingers at the employee. Focus on the conduct and not the person.

- Emphasize the behavior that is desired in the future rather than dwelling on past misconduct.

- Ask questions. Seek the employee's input as to why he or she is performing poorly.

- Listen. Be respectful of the employee's opinions, even if you disagree.

- Jointly develop strategies for improving the poor job performance. Explore with the employee how poor performance can be turned into success.

- Have a positive outlook. Let the employee know that you are confident that he or she can improve.

Employee Discipline

NOTICE OF MISCONDUCT AND OPPORTUNITY TO CHANGE

Employees who do not meet performance standards or who violate workplace rules may eventually deserve to be fired. However, good management practices require that employees be given:

- notice about their poor performance or unacceptable conduct; and
- an opportunity to make necessary changes in behavior.

This process of notice and opportunity to change is the basic structure of an effective discipline system. The purpose of discipline is not to punish an employee. Rather, effective discipline is an attempt to work with the employee to stop improper conduct. Effective discipline educates the employee about what is expected of him or her, while educating the employer about matters affecting employee conduct. Because it is fair to employees, effective discipline minimizes workforce dissatisfaction, increases productivity, boosts morale and withstands legal challenges.

BASIC STEPS OF DISCIPLINE

1. Inform the employee that he or she has engaged in specific conduct that is unacceptable and that certain conduct is expected of the employee.

2. Explain that the improper conduct must change.

3. Discuss the negative consequences that will occur if the employee fails to change unacceptable behavior and the possible positive consequences of changing the improper behavior.

4. Explore the reasons for the unacceptable behavior.

5. Develop an action plan that the supervisor and employee agree on to change the unacceptable behavior.

6. Document the disciplinary process.

✓ RULES VIOLATIONS: PRE-DISCIPLINE CHECKLIST

Before disciplining an employee for violating work rules or engaging in other workplace misconduct, ask the following questions:

☐ Did the employee have advance notice of the rule and the possible or probable disciplinary consequences of breaking the rule?

☐ Is the rule reasonably related to the orderly, efficient, and safe operation of the company?

☐ Does the rule require conduct that can be reasonably expected of the employee?

☐ Was there an investigation to determine whether the employee actually engaged in conduct that violated the rule?

☐ Was the investigation of the conduct fair and objective? Did the investigation attempt to find out the employee's version of events?

☐ Did the investigation find enough facts to show that the employee acted improperly?

☐ Has the rule in question been applied to all employees in a similar manner? Would the planned discipline be different from what was done in the case of previous violations?

☐ Does the planned "punishment" fit the "crime" in view of: (a) the seriousness of the proven misconduct; (b) the employee's record at the company; and (c) how long the employee has worked at the company?

☐ Have procedures in the company's disciplinary policy been followed? If the employee is covered by a union contract, have disciplinary procedures set forth in the contract been followed?

Don't discipline the employee if "no" is the answer to any of the above questions. Disciplining the employee when "no" is the answer to one or more of the questions can land a company in a lawsuit and make it difficult to justify the discipline in court.

COUNSEL TO IMPROVE POOR PERFORMANCE

Disciplining employees for poor performance requires a different focus than disciplining employees who violate rules or engage in misconduct. The supervisor must become more of a coach or counselor, rather than an enforcer of rules. A counseling session to improve poor performance may contain the following steps:

1. Express the performance standards for the job and review past performance of the employee. Explain why it is important to the department and the company for the employee to perform well.

2. Describe the areas of performance that the employee must improve. As much as possible, describe desired performance in terms of results that are to be achieved. Explain what happens to the department or the company when the employee does not perform well. Describe what good performance looks like.

3. Ask for the person's view on why performance does not meet standards. Does the employee believe there is a problem?

4. Discuss possible solutions. What does the person propose to do to solve the problem? Have the employee develop steps to solve the problem to create a sense of ownership in the solution. Suspend the session if the employee needs more time to develop a plan. If the employee cannot develop a plan, develop one for the employee.

5. Agree to a written action plan containing specific goals and timetables for meeting those goals.

6. Have the employee verbally commit to the action plan and provide the employee with a copy of the plan. Retain another copy as documentation of the meeting.

7. Follow up on performance based on the goals stated in the action plan. Provide feedback on how the employee is doing. Offer suggestions to improve performance. Praise instances where performance has improved.

Coaching to improve poor performance often is the first step of the progressive discipline process. However, if the employee does not improve performance, the manager will need to take more severe discipline steps.

PROGRESSIVE DISCIPLINE FOR "REPEAT OFFENDERS"

Most companies have progressive discipline systems. In a progressive discipline system, the penalty increases if misconduct is repeated or poor performance continues. Progressive discipline systems serve the goals of providing notice of unacceptable conduct and an opportunity to change. They also help to ensure that employees who engage in similar conduct are disciplined in a similar manner. Usually—but not always—the progressive discipline steps are:

1. Oral warning
2. Written warning
3. Suspension
4. Termination

Know your company's policy. Learn the company's progressive discipline policy. Be familiar with the disciplinary steps. Find out if there are any serious offenses that are exempt from the usual progressive discipline process. Understand the specific procedures that supervisors and managers must follow under the policy.

Follow your company's policy. Not following a progressive discipline policy can have serious legal consequences. For instance, failure to apply the policy to all employees who violate a rule can be used as evidence against the company in a discrimination lawsuit. Also, immediately firing an employee without following the policy's required disciplinary steps can result in the employee's suing for breach of an implied contract for continued employment.

DOCUMENT DISCIPLINARY STEPS

Documentation of discipline is essential—for both disciplinary and legal reasons. Documentation reinforces the message that a supervisor is trying to communicate in the discipline meeting. The meeting is a stressful event. The employee may not hear everything that is being said. Giving the employee a written summary of what is wrong and what must be changed will help prevent misunderstandings.

If discipline is challenged in a lawsuit, documentation allows the company to show what happened during the disciplinary process. Documentation shows when the meetings took place, what was said during the meetings, and that the employee was given notice of unacceptable behavior and an opportunity to change or improve.

AVOID INFORMAL DISCIPLINE

Supervisors must be careful with informal discipline because there is a possibility that every situation will not be treated in the same way. If one employee only gets a friendly reminder about being late while another employee gets a written warning, there is inconsistent treatment. The employee who gets the written warning may think this inconsistent treatment is based on an unlawful motive such as race or sex discrimination.

Pre-Termination Review

DON'T FIRE SOMEONE ON THE SPOT

Firing an employee on the spot can get a company into trouble. Every termination decision should be carefully reviewed for fairness, legality, and consistency with company policy. The less care that is given to making a decision to fire someone, the greater the risk the company will wind up in court. The checklists provided below are designed to help ensure that termination decisions are soundly made.

Suspension during investigation. Even if an employee has committed a serious offense that clearly calls for termination, such as hitting a coworker, it is better to suspend the employee than to immediately fire him or her. The employee should be told that he or she is suspended and must leave the premises until further contact from management. An investigation of the surrounding circumstances may uncover facts that explain the employee's behavior or make termination inappropriate.

✓ CHECKLIST: POLICY/PROCEDURE DOUBLE CHECK

☐ What specific company policy or work rule violation authorizes the termination?

☐ Where is the rule written?

☐ Is the rule reasonably related to the orderly, efficient, and safe operation of the company?

☐ Does the rule require conduct that can be reasonably expected of the employee?

☐ How do you know that the employee knew the behavior was against company rules?

☐ Has the employee had an opportunity to present his or her side of the story?

☐ Was there an investigation to determine whether the employee actually engaged in conduct that violated the rule?

☐ Was the investigation of the conduct fair and objective? Did the investigation attempt to find out the employee's version of events?

☐ Did the investigation find enough facts to show that the employee acted improperly?

☐ Did the employee have an opportunity to make necessary changes in behavior?

☐ Is termination appropriate for this infraction?

☐ Have procedures in the company's progressive discipline policy been followed?

☐ If the employee is covered by a union contract, have disciplinary procedures set forth in the contract been followed?

☐ Is termination consistent with punishment in other similar situations?

☐ Do you have authority to recommend termination or to make a termination decision?

☐ Have all persons that need to review and approve the termination action agreed with the action and signed-off?

✓ CHECKLIST: DOCUMENTATION AUDIT

• **Make sure the investigation was complete.** A complete investigation includes gathering and completing a written report of all the facts and written witness statements, including the employee's statement; preserving physical evidence and records; a review of all personnel records, including disciplinary records; and comparing actions in similar situations.

• **Prove that the termination was fair and followed company policies and practices**. Is there documentation to prove that the events were true and that company policies and procedures were followed?

• **Review the documentation.** Double check any facts cited. Make sure there are proper authorizations for all actions. Determine whether the proper forms have been used.

✓ CHECKLIST: LEGALITY REVIEW

A "yes" answer to any of the questions below is a warning sign that the planned termination may be illegal. If "yes" or "don't know" is the answer to any of these questions, consult with your Human Resources department before proceeding with the termination:

☐ Could any of the following protected categories be a factor in the recommendation to terminate the employee?

- Race or color
- Religion
- Sex
- Age
- Disability
- National origin
- Citizenship status
- Veteran or military status
- Whistleblowing
- Arrest records
- Marital status
- Sexual orientation
- State of residency
- Political affiliation
- Lawful off-duty activities

☐ Could the discharge have the appearance of discriminating on the basis of one of the above protected categories?

☐ Has the employee been a victim of abuse or harassment? Has the employee complained of abuse or harassment?

☐ Is there any reason to believe the employee may have a disability that has impaired his or her work performance?

☐ Has a request by the employee for a disability or religious accommodation been refused?

☐ Is the employee pregnant?

☐ Has the employee engaged in any political activities recently?

☐ Has the employee recently requested a military leave?

☐ Has the employee recently returned from a military leave?

☐ Has the employee engaged in union activities?

☐ Has the employee recently been called as a witness or served on jury duty?

☐ Has the employee been promised any terms or conditions of employment by anyone in a position of authority?

☐ Is the employee about to vest in any benefit?

☐ Are the employee's wages being attached or garnished?

☐ Has the employee recently been promoted, given a raise, or received a company commendation or award?

☐ Has the employee complained about wages, hours, or other work conditions?

☐ Has the employee reported company wrongdoing?

☐ Did the employee refuse to do an action because it was against the law?

☐ Has the employee filed a grievance or complaint against the company?

☐ Has the employee had medical treatment recently?

☐ Has the employee filed a workers' compensation claim?

☐ Has the employee applied for or returned from a medically-related leave of absence recently?

☐ Have false or malicious statements been made about the employee?

☐ Has personal information about the employee been revealed?

☐ Would the termination decision be any different if you knew the "facts" were to be reported in the local media?

✓ CHECKLIST: REDUCTIONS IN FORCE

☐ Be certain there is a sound business reason for reducing the size of the work force.

☐ Conduct the legality review checklist, above, before selecting employees for the workforce reduction.

☐ Have proof to back up merit-based selections.

☐ Make sure planned selections do not conflict with seniority rights under a union contract or company policy.

☐ Ensure that the planned selections do not violate employment contracts with employees.

✓ CHECKLIST: RESIGNATIONS

☐ Determine whether the employee has provided advance notice of resignation as required by company policy.

☐ Find out why the employee is leaving.

☐ If the employee has chosen to resign instead of being fired, make sure that the choice is the employee's alone and that no one has pressured the employee to resign. Also, determine whether company policy permits resignation instead of firing in the circumstances of the employee's case.

☐ Find out whether the employee is resigning in order to escape illegal or intolerable employment practices or conditions.

☐ Request that the resignation be in writing, that the reasons for resigning be stated, and that the employee sign the statement.

☐ Document the reason(s) why the employee resigned.

Conducting a Termination Meeting

WHAT SHOULD THE TERMINATION MEETING ACCOMPLISH?

One of the worst parts of any manager's or supervisor's job is telling someone that he or she has been fired or otherwise discharged from employment. It is an unpleasant and stressful task. Careful planning is required to make sure that the termination meeting efficiently communicates to the employee the termination decision and the reason for the decision. The meeting should be conducted in a manner that maintains the dignity of the person being terminated. Also, the reputation of the company as an employer that deals fairly with its people should be maintained.

The termination meeting is the last opportunity a company has to decrease the likelihood that an employee will file a lawsuit challenging the termination. To decrease potential liability, the termination meeting should be conducted in a manner that:

- Maintains the dignity of the person being terminated and minimizes as much as possible the resentment the discharged person feels toward the company.

- Explains the reason for the discharge.

According to one lawyer who represents employees who have been fired, many people who sue for wrongful discharge are trying to find out the real reason they were fired or laid off. They do not feel they were "leveled with" by management and seek out legal help to force the company to explain the "real reason" behind the termination.

WHERE TO HOLD THE MEETING

The meeting should be held privately:

- at a neutral site other than the manager's office;

- at a place with a working telephone and, preferably, at least one wall of uncovered glass; and

- in a well-lit area with at least two chairs and a desk.

WHEN TO HOLD THE MEETING

Early in the day and early in the week is the best time for conducting a termination interview. People are more relaxed, more rested, and better equipped to handle stress earlier in the day. People tend to be tired and short-tempered later in the day, and this may increase the chance for an unpleasant reaction to bad news.

SHOULD A THIRD PARTY BE THERE?

If the employee requests a witness, it is probably better to allow this so that the employee does not feel he or she is being railroaded out the door unfairly. However, explain that the witness is there only to observe the meeting, not to act as a representative for the employee's side.

A request for a union representative does not have to be granted because the purpose of the meeting is to merely inform the person of a permanent decision to discharge that has been previously made.

Management may want a third person present if trouble is expected or if an objective third person is needed. However, a second management representative may be seen as an attempt to gang up on the employee.

HAVE DOCUMENTATION AVAILABLE

The supervisor should take documentation that supports the discharge to the termination meeting. But it is not necessary to show the documentation, unless there is some misunderstanding about why the termination is occurring.

Supporting documentation might include:

- copies of relevant disciplinary rules
- performance appraisals
- memos of disciplinary meetings
- formal warnings issued during progressive discipline
- statements from witnesses gathered during the investigations
- customer complaints

WHAT TO DO DURING THE TERMINATION MEETING

The actual meeting to inform an employee that he or she is being terminated should take about 10 minutes. The purpose is to communicate that a decision has been made to terminate the employee and the reasons behind that decision. The following steps should be kept in mind when conducting the termination meeting:

1. Emphasize the following points:

    — The decision is final and cannot be reversed.

    — All relevant factors were reviewed.

    — There is agreement at all management levels.

2. Display empathy for the employee's situation but do not sympathize or become a friend to the person. If the person begins to cry, allow the expression of emotion to occur and just offer some tissue. Avoid trying to soften the bad news.

3. Don't hold out any hope that the decision will be changed or that there is a possibility for any kind of bargaining.

4. Don't "blame" the decision on upper management. Avoid making statements such as: "*They* decided to terminate your employment." Remember, you must communicate that there is agreement on the decision at all levels of management.

5. Don't lose control of the meeting or stray from the central issue of informing the person of a predetermined result. Be firm and honest, but allow the person to have his or her say. Don't interrupt or talk over the person if he or she maintains a business-like tone. If the person tries to argue with the decision, react by saying words such as: "I understand what you are saying, but the decision stands and will not be changed." If the employee becomes angry and abusive, do not respond in a similar manner. Maintain a normal tone of voice. State firmly that the meeting will not continue under such conditions.

6. Don't respond to a threat to file a lawsuit. That is the right of any person.

7. Don't discuss the situation of any other employee.

8. Communicate the reasons for the termination in factual terms. Do not make value judgments about the person's character or work ethic.

9. End the meeting by telling the person the effective date of the termination and the manner in which to leave the premises. At this point it may be appropriate

to turn the meeting over to a human resources department representative or other company official to inform the person about final payments and benefits.

SAMPLE OPENING STATEMENTS

The first moments of the termination session will often dictate the tone for the rest of the meeting. It is during this period that the supervisor can establish control of the meeting. An opening statement should be thought out and rehearsed by supervisors. The statement should first inform the employee that a termination decision has been made, followed by the reason for the termination. The tone of the statement should be non-judgmental. Words should be chosen that do not provoke a hostile reaction or invite an argument about the merits of the decision.

The following statements illustrate how a supervisor might begin a termination meeting.

Poor Performance:: Jim, we have decided to end your employment with the company. As you recall we tried several times in counseling sessions to warn you that your performance needed to improve. In the last meeting held (date) you were specifically told that failure to improve your productivity and work quality to acceptable levels could lead to termination. Unfortunately, you were unable to achieve the performance goals set out in that meeting. That inability to meet acceptable performance goals after repeated counseling and warnings is the reason we have decided to take this action. Today is your last day of employment with the company.

Attendance Problems:: Alice, I must advise you that your employment with the company is being ended effective today. We have decided to terminate your employment because of your absence and tardiness problems. You recall that we have discussed your attendance record several times in the last six months. In the written warning I gave you on (date) you were specifically informed that if you missed one more work day in a one-month period you would be terminated. Yesterday you did not show up for work and did not call to make arrangements to make up the time. Thus, I have no alternative but to follow through on the warning and terminate your employment.

References/Defamation/Privacy

WHAT IS DEFAMATION?

Defamation is a false statement—either written or spoken—about a person that harms the person's reputation. Defamation can occur when a supervisor releases inaccurate, negative information about a former employee. Critical comments made about an employee during the performance appraisal process or investigations of misconduct are also potentially defamatory. Not only can a company be held liable for defamatory statements in the workplace, so can supervisors or employees who made the statements.

WHAT ARE THE DEFENSES TO DEFAMATION?

Truth. Truth is an absolute defense to defamation claims. However, this defense will only succeed if an allegedly defamatory statement is really true. Thus, for example, a supervisor's mistaken belief that a defamatory statement about an employee is true will not satisfy the truth defense. Moreover, as discussed below, even if the statement were true, it may violate the employee's privacy rights.

Consent. Statements about an employee's performance may be protected if the employee previously consented to the disclosure. Even in the case of consent, disclosures should be limited to only those who need to know.

Qualified privilege. Managers and supervisors have a "qualified privilege" to speak openly about an issue concerning an employee with persons, such as other members of management, who have a legitimate need to know about the matter. However, the privilege will be lost if a defamatory statement is motivated by ill will or is made to or heard by persons who do not have a need to know the information. The privilege can also be lost if the statement unnecessarily includes information that is not job-related.

CASE ILLUSTRATIONS

- Distribution of a memorandum to employees attributing an employee's discharge to alcoholism, inefficiency, and unreliability was not protected by qualified privilege. The memo was distributed to employees in circumstances where a simple statement of discharge for unsatisfactory performance would have been sufficient. The employees had no business need to know the information.

- An employer's statement that an employee had been terminated for serious misconduct, including lying, was protected by qualified privilege. The statement was communicated to a state agency investigating an unemployment compensation claim. The agency was the proper party and had a business need to know the information.

WHAT IS INVASION OF PRIVACY?

Publicly disclosing private facts about an employee can result in an invasion of privacy lawsuit. Supervisors risk an invasion of privacy suit if they broadcast matters such as the details of a performance evaluation, the reasons for disciplining or firing an employee, an employee's medical test results, or an employee's sexual orientation. Although truth is a defense to defamation claims, it is not a defense to an invasion of privacy claim.

TIPS FOR AVOIDING DEFAMATION/PRIVACY CLAIMS

- Don't discuss disciplinary or performance issues concerning an employee except with persons who have a legitimate right to know. Make sure the discussion is in a private area and cannot be overheard. Stick to the topic at hand—don't discuss unrelated information about the employee.

- Carefully investigate suspected employee performance or discipline problems before reaching any conclusions.

- Make sure that any employment decision made with respect to an employee is objective and well-founded. Do not base any decision on rumor or malicious statements.

- Caution employees who report misconduct by a coworker of the risk of personal defamation liability if they make malicious or false statements or discuss the matter with others. Whenever possible, obtain a written statement from them.

- Never be petty, malicious, or dishonest when talking about an employee or documenting information about the employee.

- Don't document information about an employee that has no clear business purpose.

- When documenting the reasons for an employee's discipline or termination, stick to the facts. Don't include unnecessary information or personal comments. Don't make matters sound worse than they are.

- Check existing employee records for accuracy and completeness. Remove any unnecessary information.

- Keep documentation on employees strictly confidential. Lock file cabinets where employee records are kept. When sending records, make sure they are well-sealed and marked "confidential." Use all available security protections when transmitting computerized records.

- At the time of an employee's exit interview, explain the company's reference procedures to the employee and then obtain a written consent for release of information.

- Never publicly disclose private facts about an employee. Don't broadcast the details of a performance evaluation, the reasons for disciplining or firing an employee, medical information about an employee, an employee's sexual orientation, etc.

HOW TO EXPLAIN WHY A COWORKER WAS FIRED

If an employee asks why a coworker was fired, first tell the employee that the company treats all such personnel matters as confidential. Next, check company policy. If company policy allows any explanation, only give a very general response. For example, if the coworker was fired for theft, do not say the person was fired for stealing. Instead, say the person was terminated for failure to follow company policy and procedure. Specific details should not be disclosed.

In a few cases, a supervisor may believe that employees have a need to know the details. The supervisor should have a very solid reason for wanting to disclose the information. For example, disclosure may be necessary for health or safety reasons. In such cases, assuming company policy allows disclosure, the communication should be accurate and limited in scope. Discuss the facts in an objective, nonmalicious way and avoid making accusatory statements.

HOW TO HANDLE JOB REFERENCE REQUESTS

Check company policy. Always check company policy before responding to any reference check. Find out who has authority to give references. Determine what may be said in a reference. Many companies prohibit managers and supervisors from giving references and require that references be forwarded to the Human Resources department. Companies usually limit what may be said in a reference to the dates of employment, job title last held, and what the job duties were.

Find out who you are talking to. Make sure that you are talking with someone who has an interest in knowing the information—usually someone who wants to hire your former employee. Ask for the caller's name, title, company and phone number. Also, ask if the caller has a written authorization from the former employee to acquire the information.

Make sure requests are in writing. Ask the caller to submit the request in writing. Even if your company allows managers and supervisors to respond to a reference check, no response should be given unless the request is in writing.

Avoid "off-the-record" comments. Don't be tricked into responding to someone who promises to keep the requested information strictly in confidence.

Be neutral. If your company has no policy on what managers and supervisors may say in a job reference, the best practice to follow is to provide only the dates of employment, the job title last held, and a description of the job duties. Regardless of whether a person was a good or poor employee, no further information should be given.

Be accurate. If you are required to provide a reference, provide only truthful, job-related information based on proper documentation. Never provide misleading information. For example, in the case of an employee with a known dangerous propensity (i.e., documented violent behavior), do not provide a favorable reference.

Take notes. Keep notes when someone calls for a reference about a former employee for placement in the personnel file reflecting the date, caller, nature of the inquiry, position applied for, questions asked by the caller, and information given.

SPECIAL CONFIDENTIALITY RULES FOR MEDICAL RECORDS

Federal laws require that all medical information from employees be collected on separate forms, kept in separate medical files, and treated as a confidential medical record. Medical information must never be placed in an employee's personnel file. The information should be kept in a separate, locked cabinet apart from the location of personnel files. Disclosure of the information is allowed only in the following circumstances:

- Supervisors and managers may be told of necessary restrictions on an employee's work or duties and necessary accommodations.

- First aid and safety personnel may be told if an employee's medical condition might require emergency treatment.

- Relevant information may be given on request to government agents investigating law compliance, workers' compensation offices, or insurance companies.

Notes

Notes

Notes

Notes